D0852236

EVERYTHING I EVER NEEDED
TO KNOW ABOUT **ECONOMICS**
I LEARNED FROM
ONLINE DATING

EVERYTHING I EVER NEEDED
TO KNOW ABOUT **ECONOMICS**
I LEARNED FROM
ONLINE DATING

PAUL OYER

HARVARD BUSINESS REVIEW PRESS

BOSTON, MASSACHUSETTS

The web addresses referenced in this book were live and correct at the time of the book's publication but may be subject to change.

Library of Congress Cataloging-in-Publication Data

Oyer, Paul E. (Paul Edward), 1963-
  Everything I ever needed to know about economics I learned from online dating / Paul Oyer.
     pages cm
    ISBN 978-1-4221-9165-1 (hardback)
1. Online dating—Economic aspects. 2. Economics—Sociological aspects. 3. Economics—Psychological aspects. I. Title.
  HQ801.82.O94 2014
  306.730285—dc23

                    2013029760

IN MEMORY OF MY MOTHER

CONTENTS

EVERYTHING I EVER NEEDED TO KNOW ABOUT **ECONOMICS** I LEARNED FROM ONLINE DATING

INTRODUCTION

It was a crisp fall evening, and I was sitting at a table outside Cafe Borrone near my house in the heart of Silicon Valley, awaiting the arrival of my first date in over twenty years. A lot had happened in that time. For example, within a twenty-five mile radius of the cafe, engineers had transformed our lives dramatically by developing the internet. At a more personal level, I had become an economist and was now a professor teaching and researching my field.

As I waited, I realized how the rise of the internet had led me to my seat at the cafe. The internet not only created Facebook, eBay, and Amazon—it has also transformed the dating scene. In 1990, "dating services" existed, but they were generally looked down on. Many, probably most, people (including me) thought that only the desperate used dating services. But thanks to the internet, which made communication so easy, many people had turned to online dating by 2010.

It also hit me that internet dating itself is largely economics—and I was in a much better position to understand that than I was when I was last on the "market." For the last twenty years, as the internet transformed the economy, I've spent at least part of almost every day analyzing markets. Suddenly, I was thrust into one of the most interesting markets there is. Match.com, eHarmony, and OkCupid, it turns out, are no different from eBay or Monster.com. On all these sites, people come together trying to find matches. Sure, there are a lot of differences between someone selling a used bowling ball on eBay and someone signing up for Match.com, but the basic idea is the same. The bowler needs to think about how to present his bowling ball to get what he wants (money, presumably) just as the Match.com participant needs to present himself to get what he wants (a partner in most cases, casual sex in others). It's really not that different.

And after spending twenty years learning about and studying markets, as well as watching them develop in the modernizing "information economy," I had suddenly been thrust back into one of the most fascinating markets that exists—the market for life partners. The models I had been studying and researching were no longer abstract ideas or objective statistics. I became a player in the market, thinking about how all the ideas economists study were driving my behavior and the behavior of all the other people on dating websites.

Granted, online dating is a very complicated market because, unlike stock markets or gold markets, the items being traded are not commodities. There are no perfect substitutes in this market—each item is different. Also, no money trades hands.[1] This lack of money may make the dating market not seem like a market at all, but eighteen years of economics training has allowed me to see economics everywhere. And no place has more economics than online dating sites.

Hopefully, by the end of this book, you too will be seeing economics everywhere in today's modern information economy. In the next ten chapters, I hope to explain key microeconomic concepts to anyone who wants to learn a little economics—ideas that are fundamental to how the modern economy works and increasingly to our personal lives as well: search, signaling, adverse selection, cheap talk, statistical discrimination, thick markets, and network externalities. These ideas are all driving the behavior of online dating participants every day, and that unique market is where I'll start each chapter.

I'll appeal to examples from my own experiences (that first date at Cafe Borrone and many that followed did not work out, so I have plenty of others to draw from) and from stories I've read and heard from others. Each chapter will go on to explain how this same economic idea plays out in other places such as the labor market, eBay, or buying a house—that is, you'll learn the economics that drive the world through the lens of online dating.

---

1. I know what you're thinking. Yes, plenty of money trades hands in markets for partners. But most people involved in online dating are not buying or selling sex. I will not touch on the prostitution market or sex trade at all in this book. Sorry.

My hope is that you will learn a lot about economics and how the modern world works by reading the pages ahead, and that you'll have a good time doing so. I also hope that you'll find at least some of the information useful if you ever use an online dating site, although I find it a little hard to imagine I could ever help anyone looking for love.[2] But you never know.

---

2. If you do learn something useful along these lines, please invite me to the wedding. I hardly ever get the chance to go to weddings anymore.

1

SEARCH THEORY

Deciding When to Settle

Many people believe there exists a single person who is their perfect partner or "soul mate." That may be true, but then I certainly hope that my soul mate does not live in a remote village in India. Suppose that my soul mate was born, like me, in the 1960s. Limiting myself to women who are still alive, and assuming that half of them have already met their soul mates, I have perhaps 200 million potential partners. If I meet two potential partners a day, there's a 50/50 chance I will find my soul mate within a quarter of a million years.

OK, the strategy of meeting every woman I can until I find my soul mate doesn't sound too promising. So what's my best alternative? If I accept that I won't meet "the one," when should I think I've met the best one available, given the amount of time and effort I can reasonably allocate to looking for a partner?

Let's start by thinking of a day in my life. At the time of this writing, I am not seeing anyone seriously. So here is a partial list of things I hoped to accomplish today when I woke up this morning: meet (or at least connect with) my next life partner, do some analysis for an academic paper that I am working on, do the *New York Times* crossword puzzle, get updated on the news through the newspaper and NPR, eat something truly delicious, exercise, spend some quality time with my children, walk my dog, and practice the piano. I could actually go on and on, but let's start there.

The more of those things I accomplish today, the happier I will be when I go to sleep tonight. In economist terms, doing more of those things (and, if I'm lucky, having some other unexpected good things happen) will make my *utility* higher when I go to bed tonight. As I go through my day, I'm making thousands of little decisions. What will I eat? Should I play that piano piece one more time? Should I run one more regression, or am I convinced my economics paper is correct? Each one is driven implicitly by what I think will make me happiest.

I will often have to make decisions that will affect my utility in unpredictable ways, though, so some of my end-of-day utility will be higher or lower than I expect when I decide what to do.

So now consider me, sitting in front of my computer screen, reviewing profiles on OkCupid or inspecting the e-mails that OkCupid sends me suggesting particular women. I spend quite a bit of time doing such perusing, as well as contacting and following up with women. To be perfectly honest, I would rather not do that. I have a lot of other things I would rather do (or feel I should do) with my time, as you may remember from my ambitious list of plans. But I will review another profile if I think the additional utility from the chance that that person will become my life partner outweighs the additional utility I will get from using the time in some other manner.

This idea of *utility* is simultaneously one of the most abstract and intuitively appealing concepts in economics. It's just an economist's way to keep score of how happy someone is. If I have a satisfying long-term relationship, or even a good first date, that makes me happy—it increases my utility. So I spend time on OkCupid in the hope that I will meet someone who will someday increase my utility.

We are all constantly making decisions that maximize our expected utility. You are, in fact, doing this as we speak; at some level, you're asking yourself if you would be happier if you continued reading this book than you would be if you put it down and did something else. Notice that I said you are maximizing your *expected* utility. This is because you have to make some choices when you are uncertain about how they will pay off. You may regret them later, but you essentially are making a lot of best guesses about how your decisions in the present will impact your utility in the future.

Search models in economics analyze the trade-offs that people face regularly when deciding whether to accept the best option available or to keep looking. In the online dating world, this means I know that looking at one more profile creates some chance that this person will turn out to be the absolute love of my life and will make me happier than any woman ever could. When I think of it that way, I almost feel a *responsibility* to go look at another profile. How can I sit here writing this book when the very next woman I look at on Match.com could be the best match for me? But we all know that logic like that doesn't work—we don't spend an unlimited amount of time looking for a perfect match.

We *settle*. There, I said it. You don't want to admit it. You love your mate and think he or she is the greatest. Or, if you are still looking, you are hoping you will find someone "perfect." But you won't. I don't want to burst your bubble, but you just are not going to find the perfect match. Even if he or she is out there, you almost definitely won't find that person. At some point, you will say to yourself (though I recommend you do not say this out loud), "My partner is truly wonderful. If I kept looking, I could probably do better. But I have to earn a living, make dinner, practice the piano, and do a bunch of other stuff. So I'm going to settle for this person and move on with life. It could certainly be a lot worse."

The decision of when to stop searching actually happens at every stage of the online dating process. First, there's the question of whether you should look at one more profile or not. Next comes the decision of whether to have a second date, a third date, and so on, or to search for an alternative potential partner. Then, when you've been seeing someone for a while, you must decide whether to commit to seeing only that person, maybe move in, and eventually marry—or whether to return to the market and try again. Finally, even when you are in a long-term relationship, you will constantly be deciding whether the relationship you have is better than the alternative of breaking it off and trying for a better one.

Hopefully, that thought won't be very explicit in your mind, but throughout your relationship you will be implicitly choosing what you have over what you could find elsewhere.

You may be thinking that analyzing the dating market this way is something only an economist would do, and that real daters don't behave this way. But Nick Paumgarten, in researching a long essay on online dating for the *New Yorker*, spoke to a wide array of online daters in the process. He discovered an entire class of people who look to "trade up"—in other words, "see someone until someone better comes along." He writes, "When there is something better out there, you can't help trying to find it."

Another take on when it is time to trade up was provided by the Miranda Hobbes character on *Sex and the City* who said, "I'm living with skid-marks guy . . . When your boyfriend is so comfortable that he cannot be bothered to wipe his ass, that's the end of romance, right there."

Who Keeps Looking for a Better Partner?

So, who settles for what they have, and who keeps going?

To an economist, there is one set of people who are surely less likely to settle down—those whose *search costs* are lowest. In the online dating world, this concept can mean a few different things. First, there are some people who just plain like (or at least don't much mind) searching. They enjoy looking at online dating sites the way some people enjoy looking at catalogs, browsing in stores and malls, or spending a weekend afternoon antiquing. These people have no reason to settle down. To them, there is too much utility in the hunt.

Paumgarten found at least a few of these people, who, he says, think "internet dating can be a sport, an end in itself." I don't happen to be one of these people, though—I don't like poring over online dating sites and, as I have already noted, there are a lot of other things I want to do with my time.

Which leads to the second group of people who will not settle down—those who have nothing better to do than look at internet dating sites. Everything else being equal, if you have no hobbies and no particularly good way to make money—if you have some spare time and you generally spend a lot of it sitting around bored—then you will keep looking for the perfect mate. But "everything else being equal" is really important in this case. The person I just described may be very choosy because he has nothing else to do, but the very thing that makes him choosy also makes him less attractive to others. So not only is someone who has nothing better to do than search for the perfect match going to want to keep looking, he's also not going to have much choice. In this case, the factor that makes the person keep looking because he can do better (which, in economics terminology, is the low cost of his time) is the thing that will likely make him less attractive, and so he will have no choice but to keep looking. We will get into this idea of *adverse selection* in more detail in chapter 7.

Having nothing better to do or enjoying the hunt makes people reluctant to settle because hunting is not costly to them. But people might also be more reluctant to settle if they perceive the benefits of continuing the search to be high enough. That is, if someone thinks he really can expect to get a better mate from continued search, then he won't settle just yet.

So who gets the most from trading up? Well, frankly, picky people. If all I really wanted was company—someone to come home to, someone to spend time with—I would go on a date and, as long as the person didn't dump me, I would accept the person and settle down pretty quickly. Why try to trade up if most potential mates are good enough?

I don't know that I'm any pickier than the next guy, but I do have specific tastes. For example, it is really important that my partner laugh a lot at my jokes. I can't tell from an online profile, or even from a first date, if someone is going to laugh at my jokes. I have to get to know the person pretty well. From a lot of interactions with colleagues, friends, and former dates and girlfriends, I have a pretty good idea of how much a typical person laughs at my jokes (not much) and how many people laugh a lot at them (not many). I know that, if I want to find someone who is a real champion at enjoying my jokes, I have to try a lot of people. It might take me a while to find such a woman, and I have to keep searching after most interactions.

That would be bad enough, but, in addition to a partner who laughs at my jokes, I want a partner to make a lot of good jokes of her own, be able to discuss current political events with me in an interesting and open-minded way, and enjoy the same types of movies I enjoy. And, of course, she has to understand that I will spend a lot of time with my teenage children and my large and badly behaved dog. The fraction of the single female population that ranks highly on all those dimensions is very low. If I go on several dates with someone I like whom I've met on OkCupid, the odds are very low that she will rate highly in every one of those dimensions.

It turns out there are people out there who are a lot choosier than I am. A graduate student in China created an online dating profile that listed the following traits she was looking for: "Never married; master's degree or more; not from Wuhan; no rural ID card; no only children; no smokers; no alcoholics; no gamblers; taller than one hundred and seventy-two centimeters; more than a year of dating before marriage; sporty; parents who are still together; annual salary over fifty thousand yuan; between twenty-six and thirty-two years of age; willing to guarantee eating four dinners at home per week; at least two ex-girlfriends, but no more than four; no Virgos. No Capricorns." It's too bad I didn't see this ad when I was about twenty-eight years old, as I actually met her criteria at that time (except for one little secret that I will reveal later).

What should I do if I go on a few dates with a woman and find that, while we get along well, she does not meet all my criteria? Maybe she likes horror movies, for example. Or what if the Chinese woman meets a man who is 171 centimeters or is a Virgo? In those cases, should we give up and start all over?

The answer, of course, depends on how much happier adding the missing attributes would be relative to the time spent starting all over. It pays to be tolerant. If the Chinese woman or I lower our standards along any of the dimensions, we could settle down faster and avoid further search costs.

This logic leads to yet another group of people who are less likely to settle for a given person and more likely to keep looking—those who are patient. Imagine two men—let's call them Bryan and Carl—looking for women to settle down with. These guys are exactly the same on all dimensions, except that Carl is very patient. He thinks about his future a lot and plans his life with the long term in mind. Carl saves more of his income than Bryan, who is more likely to go out and blow money on a nice car. A person like Carl is also more likely to be picky in choosing life partners. Bryan is tempted to save himself the short-term trouble of looking more (and being lonely while he looks), even if it means he ends up with a less ideal partner for the rest of his life. Carl's patience leads to pickiness. With any luck, this will pay off in a better match for him someday, but today he pays the price in loneliness.

Returning to me and the very picky Chinese woman, I have more incentive to settle for someone who does not meet all my criteria than she does. I should be more impatient because, being a little bit older, I have less time to spend with my next mate. So I should value the present more than the future, at least relative to the young Chinese woman, because I don't have as much future to value.

How Do I Know When to Settle?

Economists generally believe that every single person is making the best decision he or she can, given the information available, to determine when to settle. Some people make mistakes, of course, by settling too soon (leading to divorce) or not soon enough (leading to growing old alone, lamenting not having settled down with some ex-partner when the chance was there). But as long as each person is doing his or her best to maximize utility at any given time, most people will get a good match at some point.

Some people who are not generally thinking of this in terms of economics would argue that people are simply bad utility maximizers. That is, that people are not willing to settle when they should and that, as a result, there are a lot of single people who miss their chance to have children. This category most often applies to women who feel their biological clocks ticking but resist the temptation to lower their standards in men too much just for the sake of starting a family.

Author Lori Gottlieb is one proponent of the "women don't know how to maximize their utility" camp (though I doubt she would ever put it in those terms). She wrote, "My advice is this: Settle! That's right. Don't worry about passion or intense connection . . . Based on my observations, in fact, settling will probably make you happier in the long run." She advocates being very picky about the qualities that truly matter—honesty, kindness, generosity, shared values—and letting go of those that don't. As an eligible man, I read this and say, "Right on! You tell them." As an economist, though, I read that last sentence of hers and I want to reword it: "Women underestimate the loss of utility in being single and can improve their lifetime utility by settling for a man they would otherwise think was below their standards."

Gottlieb goes on to use Jane, Holly Hunter's character in the movie *Broadcast News*, as an example. She questions whether Jane will someday regret rejecting "smart, funny, and kind" Aaron (Albert Brooks). "She loves Aaron deeply, but she doesn't feel any fireworks," Gottlieb explains. Instead, Jane pines for the "handsome but shallow" Tom

(William Hurt). An economist would assume that Jane had made rational choices throughout the process and, whatever comes of her love life, she had every reason to think she would be happier by rejecting Aaron. Gottlieb points out that there is no reason to think Jane made the right choice and that, at least for a typical woman, just going ahead and marrying Aaron would have been the better choice. I suspect that Gottlieb would advise the woman who would not date a Virgo to significantly pare down her list of requirements.

Many people have (again, without putting it in these exact terms) taken the "women can maximize their utility just fine" position in rebutting Gottlieb's view. One user of a forum on Plentyoffish (a dating site) wrote, "I can force myself to eat a salad because it's good for me. But how am I supposed to make conversation with a loser for twenty years in a row?" Another online comment suggested, essentially, that Gottlieb should worry about maximizing her own utility and not tell others how to increase theirs: "I tire of articles that write a broad script of how women should be handling their personal and professional lives. Speak for yourself, instead of evangelizing quiet desperation for security."

I am not going to tell you whether or when to settle—I leave it to you to maximize your own utility. Gottlieb may or may not be right that more women should settle. But, regardless of whether people are too picky, one thing is for sure when you search for a partner, or for almost anything else: whether or not you are perfectly rational, search theory says that there is definitely a chance that you will regret passing up a chance you had.

OK, I Found a Mate—How Do I Find a House?

The same exact logic, with one important twist, applies when buying a house. Let's say I want a house that has a nice view, four bedrooms, two baths, modern architecture, and is within five miles of my office. Oh, and I need it to be in good shape, because I am not very handy. I start dropping in on open houses, I search house profiles on internet realty sites (I told you the logic was going to be similar to finding a partner), maybe I even get a realtor to show me a few places. Pretty soon I've seen a *lot* of houses, and each one is pretty nice. But none of them has every single thing I wanted. Do I keep looking? Or do I settle? The cost of looking at another house is not trivial. I have to drive over there and I have to give up something else I'd like to do with my time. But that next house . . . It might be *the one*.

The things that might make me settle for a house are the same as those that lead me to settle on a mate. If I like looking at houses, if I have nothing better to do with my weekends than go to open houses, or if I'm really picky (that is, I just cannot be happy in a house with tile I don't like even if the house is otherwise a match), then I will keep looking until I find the perfect house.

But there is, as I mentioned, a big difference between a house and a life partner. The house does not have to love me back—it doesn't "choose" me. I get the house if I have enough money, whereas I only get the life partner of my choice if she settles for me. That matters a lot in terms of the details of my actions during the courtship process—I dress better for dates than I dress when I go house hunting, for example. But it matters even more in terms of deciding when to settle.

When picking a life partner, I don't get to pick the best one available. I get to pick the best one available who picks me back. In this way, the online dating search process is much more similar to the job search process than it is to the house hunting process.

Unemployment: The Labor Market's Loneliness

The parallels between searching for a job and searching for a partner are striking. In both cases, there is a two-sided search process going on, in which both parties are considering all their options. Both sides of the "market" find it costly to go out and look for a partner (or, in the job context, an employee or employer) and both sides know that, if they keep looking, something better might become available. So people looking for jobs are reluctant to settle, just as people looking for partners are. And in both cases, there is a substantial penalty for being picky: life partner seekers who refuse to settle end up lonely; job seekers who refuse to settle end up unemployed.

That key insight—the possibility that, if I hold out just a bit longer, I might get a better job offer—has led to a huge stream of economics research. Two of the most prolific contributors to that literature, Dale Mortensen and Christopher Pissarides, won the Nobel Prize for their pioneering work on search costs and the labor market. In announcing the prize, the Nobel committee declared, "Since the search process requires time and resources, it creates frictions in the market. On such search markets, the demands of some buyers will not be met, while some sellers cannot sell as much as they would wish. Simultaneously, there are both job vacancies and unemployment on the labor market."

In the end, loneliness—that biggest fear that leads us to online dating and, eventually, settling for a less-than-ideal mate—is no more than romantic unemployment. Search frictions slow down the matching process in labor markets, leading to people being unemployed or underemployed. Similarly, search frictions lead people to be lonely because, though a really great partner may be out there, we don't know how to find each other.

Search Engines Lower Search Costs

When you do a Google search or use Gmail, advertisements pop up related to your search or e-mail conversation. Google makes fabulous amounts of money on these keyword searches because they have proven effective at matching advertisers to people interested in their products. This entire business is based on the importance of search costs—not the search engine's costs, but your costs of searching for something.

Sometimes I take a break from searching for my next life partner and search for other more mundane things I need. I was recently looking for a new nonstick skillet on which to inflict my mediocre cooking skills. I entered "nonstick skillet" into Google and was given a list of links based on Google's search algorithms. In addition, I was presented with three sponsored links at the top of the web page and several more on a column on the right side of the page, each of which would take me to websites that have to pay Google some amount of money if I click on them. An auction determines the placement of links—the company that bids the most wins the right to be the first to offer me its nonstick skillet.

Why is someone willing to pay more to be the top link on the page? Why not bid a little less and settle for being the second link? Because, like most people, I search as little as possible in order to avoid spending my lunch hour comparing qualities of nonstick skillets. Thus, I am more likely to click on the top link. It's that simple. The top link is a bit easier to see and more prominent, so I am more likely to click on it. In other words, search theory suggests that I (like other people) am lazy, and bidders on sponsored links are willing to pay to take advantage of my laziness.

While search costs are important online, the difference between the price of the best- and second-best-placed sponsored links is typically not all that great. The internet has reduced consumers' search costs dramatically, so shoppers can quickly follow a few different sponsored links to compare, for example, Williams-Sonoma's nonstick skillet offerings to Crate & Barrel's. However, search costs are much greater in the physical shopping world, where I would have to drive around (or at least call around) to compare skillets.

Economist Alan Sorensen showed the importance of search costs in the market for pharmaceuticals at local pharmacies. Sorensen's analysis relies on the fact that people act quite differently when buying a diabetes drug that they have to take daily for an extended period of time relative to how they act when they buy an antibiotic for short-term treatment of an infection. Just as the younger Chinese woman should be a lot more picky than I should be about choosing our next mates, the diabetic drug consumer has a lot more to gain by shopping around to determine who has the best price on the pills he will consume for years and years than does the person with an infection.

So what does this mean for the pharmacies when they set their prices of the two drugs? The pharmacy manager knows that the prices on the diabetes drug cannot be too high, because those consumers are going to do some comparison shopping. But with the antibiotic, he might think to himself, "If I set a high price, a lot of people are just going to buy it and not notice." He can't go crazy with his antibiotic price because some people have a lot of time on their hands and they will shop around for any drug—if his prices were too aggressive, his pharmacy would become known for price gouging. But overall, we would expect to see higher *margins* (that is, a higher price to the consumer relative to what the pharmacy pays) on the antibiotic than on the diabetes drug. We would also expect different pharmacies to try different strategies on pricing the antibiotic drug; some would attempt to be more aggressive while others would try to cater to the customers who shop around even on infrequently purchased items. On the other hand, prices of the diabetes drug will be very similar across pharmacies because more consumers shop around before buying that item.

To figure out the importance of search costs, Sorensen took advantage of the fact that New York State requires pharmacies to publicly post the prices they charge for certain prescription drugs. He drove around upstate New York, writing down the prices posted in the stores (and getting strange looks from pharmacy employees). Sure enough, he found that profit margins were noticeably higher for infrequently purchased items, such as antibiotics, than for frequent purchases, such as diabetes drugs. The typical pharmacy knew it could get away with a bit more markup on a drug that the sick person would only buy once. Sorensen also found that prices are much more similar from pharmacy to pharmacy on drugs where consumers have more incentive to shop around. Diabetes drug prices were very similar from one pharmacy to the next—pharmacists figure out that they won't sell much if they veer from the going rate.

I'll Get a Better Deal When I Get Old

Just as we have more incentive to shop around more for an item we will purchase regularly and repeatedly, we also have more incentive to carefully find the best deal at different times of our lives. One manifestation of this is that, once you are older and retired, you will have more time to look for a good deal. Just to pick a random example, think about a single father of two teenagers who has to teach two classes the next day that he is unprepared for and who has promised the editor of his in-progress book that he would soon deliver a draft of an as-yet-unwritten chapter. While driving home one night to feed his kids and shuttle them around, he notices that he needs gas and passes a filling station. He hasn't given a lot of thought to the price of gas lately, but the price at this station strikes him as high and he thinks that, by driving a few extra miles, he can save a few dollars at another filling station.

Now let's move this same single father forward in time ten or twenty years. His kids no longer live at home (let's

Dosh!

hope not, anyway) and he's not feeling as much pressure to produce books. He may even have retired from teaching and, if not, he's taught the class so many times that he really doesn't need a great deal of preparation time. Suppose he passes a gas station and has the same thought—that the price looks a bit high and he may be able to do better at the station a few miles away.

Which version of our friend is more likely to drive to the other filling station? The older version, of course, because the value of his time is lower and he gives up less in his quest to save a few dollars. Economists Mark Aguiar and Erik Hurst carefully studied this age-based difference in the cost of searching and documented large differences in shopping patterns. They showed that the price paid for a typical good is constant for people through the end of middle age, and then it drops quickly and substantially. A person in her late forties pays, on average, 4 percent more for the same product than her neighbor in his late sixties.

Aguiar and Hurst show that some of these senior savings come from discounts (coupons, membership cards, etc.), which is one form of searching for a better deal. But they also show that some of the price difference is driven by older people spending a lot more time shopping than younger people. Rest assured, Aguiar and Hurst did not follow a lot of people around, keeping track of how much time they spent shopping. They used the American Time Use Survey, which gets thousands of people to record how they spend all of one twenty-four hour period. Aguiar and Hurst found that people between the ages of sixty-five and seventy-four spend about a third more time shopping than people aged forty-five to forty-nine and 50 percent more time shopping than people aged twenty-five to twenty-nine.

Of course, Aguiar and Hurst might come to different conclusions if they redid their study. They used data gathered in the mid-1990s, before the large-scale rise of the internet (and certainly before the senior citizen set was using the internet). But now, perhaps Aguiar and Hurst would find that lots of seniors (especially the widows and widowers) were so busy scouring SeniorFriendFinder.com that they had no time to look for bargains when they shop. They may be too busy maximizing their expected utility in other ways.

Some Things to Take Away from Chapter 1

A Key Insight from Economics: Because the act of searching is costly, people often cannot find exactly what they are looking for even when it is out there somewhere. As a result, many perfectly eligible and attractive people are single, some great potential employees are unemployed, and some really nice houses sit empty and unsold.

A Valuable or Important Empirical Finding by Economists Who Study Search Costs: Retailers are in a better position to gouge consumers on items they buy infrequently. You can count on the market to force the price of fairly standard products to be competitive, but you'd better shop around if you don't want to overpay for specialty items.

When It Comes to Search Theory, Dating Is a Lot Like:
Buying a house, looking for a job, deciding which station
to go to when you need gas.

Dating Advice: At some point, stop, and, in the words of
Stephen Stills, "Love the one you're with."

2

Game Theory Subsection

CHEAP TALK

Hedges, Omissions, and Just Plain Lies

"If you had the real thing, how would you tell? Liars can
say it all just as well. Every single word you've heard
in vain . . . one hundred love letters and none of them true."

—"Christina" by Patty Griffin

"This is like writing a résumé and trying to be
honest . . . but not TOO honest :) . . . "

—A woman's "self-summary" on OkCupid

When I set up my profile on Match.com, I tried to tell the
truth, and I mostly succeeded. For example, I was up-front
about my teenage children and my sweet but impish golden
retriever. But I left out the YouTube videos my children
introduced me to under "Things I Find Entertaining," and

checked the "Never" box when asked how often I smoke, despite the fact that I have never fully shaken my futile attempts to be cool.

I admit it—I lied.

There are people who do not exaggerate at all on their dating profiles and hold back no particle of truth. And there are Match.com profiles that put my mischaracterizations to shame. (If I had a nickel for every overweight person who describes him- or herself as "Athletic and Toned," or every cynic who claims a positive outlook on life, I would have a lot of nickels.) No one is immune to the temptation to exaggerate a bit—I know one very nice seventy-two-year-old widow who claimed to be sixty-nine on her Match.com profile.

But what led me to be honest on some parts of my profile and not others? And what leads some online daters to be paragons of truth?

We can find the answer in a branch of game theory known as *cheap talk*.

A cheap talk framework considers the potential conflict between my preferences and those of the women I am trying to attract and lets us analyze, in a given situation, when and if it is sensible to hide information or lie outright. Since what was true about me and what I thought would appeal to people I hoped would want to meet me were often the same, I could quickly and thoroughly fill in most answers as I created my profile. But sometimes there was a conflict between an honest answer and what I thought would make me attractive to the women I wanted to be attractive *to*. *Game theory* would say it all came down to utility: the degree to which I was truthful and forthcoming depended on what I was looking for in people, what I *thought* the people I wanted to meet were looking for, and the probable cost to me of lying about myself.

Game theory typically addresses situations in which, when one party wins, the other loses. That's where strategy comes in. But *cooperative* game theory models what happens when the interests of the parties are perfectly aligned, as in some online dating, where both users would like to find long-term partners. For a cooperative model of online dating to fully work, nobody would have anything at all to hide, and all would-be daters would reveal as much as they possibly could. That means the women who were most attractive to me would be exactly the same women who would be most attracted to my completely honest, fully informative online profile.

Ah, well. As much as we would all love to be loved for the people we are, things are more complicated. A woman and I can find each other attractive, but at the same time, she finds my favorite internet video extremely unfunny. Or that same woman could feel she could never go out with anyone who smoked. If I revealed my video and occasional smoke on my profile, that woman would never agree to meet me in the first place.

So I make an executive decision. I, like many others, hide these minutiae. I rationalize that, even if a woman eventually finds these things out after we're in a deeper relationship, she'll accept these small negative traits as part of the whole package. And I justify my minor deception by arguing I'm doing myself *and* the woman a favor. It's cooperative game theory. Our interests are aligned, and I've simply removed some minor hurdles.

Lying Online? Really?

As I said, I know from my own experiences that many people lie about their looks and their positive attitude when they set up a dating profile. And my experience is not unusual, as research shows that lying is prevalent on dating sites.

Jeffrey Hancock, Catalina Toma, and Nicole Ellison contacted people who had posted online dating profiles to verify the information they provided. They found that most men exaggerated their height, most people of both gender understated their weight, and about one-fifth of people lied about their age. Most of the deception was relatively minor, though, with a typical person claiming to be an inch taller, about five pounds lighter, and a year or two younger. Very few people tried bold lies—which is what we would expect, given that anything so obvious would be so easily detected at the first meeting.

OkCupid's blog provided further evidence on the degree of lying in dating profiles. It found that the average heights claimed by men on their profiles are suspiciously greater than the average height of American men and that there are an inexplicable number of men who claim to be exactly six feet tall. Similarly, it found that the incomes claimed on the site are equally suspicious—there are four times as many people making $100,000 per year as there should be. Finally, they found that people often posted dated pictures that likely made them look more attractive than they really were. More specifically, they reached the very scientific finding that "hotter photos were much more likely to be outdated than normal ones."

A Few Liars Ruin It for Everyone

What is going through the minds of people who misrepresent themselves online by claiming to be younger, taller, or more attractive than they really are?

Take the extreme (and imaginary) case of Roger, an unattractive, unpleasant, and unemployed man. Roger wants to date supermodels. Pretty much without exception, all supermodels prefer successful and attractive men to Roger. Roger cannot post a fully revealing and honest profile on Match.com, because then none of the women he wants to attract will contact him or reply favorably when he contacts them.

Instead, Roger simply fabricates a description. He says he is rich, describes how much fun he is to be with, and posts pictures of male models instead of pictures of himself.

But a person smart enough to think this strategy through quickly sees that it could never pay off. Once Roger met a supermodel in person, she would simply end the date. (NB: there's an iPhone "Fake-A-Call" app online daters use for just such situations.) Thus Roger accepts that he cannot date supermodels by lying on his profile. Instead, he settles for something less than his ideal woman. But he'd still like to get the best woman he can.

Roger is now left with an interesting problem—how to make himself seem as attractive as possible without telling any lies so blatant that *any* woman who agrees to a date with him won't end it immediately. It's a delicate balance, but he eventually figures out just how much lying he can get away with so that the most desirable women he can manage won't leave immediately when he walks in the door.

Unfortunately, Roger's lies, and the lies those like Roger tell, have major ramifications for those of us who would like to tell the truth. Roger's lies and the lies of others lead all of us to discount claims on profiles as cheap talk.

For instance, everybody knows that many people who claim to be "Athletic and Toned" on Match.com are closer to the "A Few Extra Pounds" category. Why do they lie? Because profile-inflaters like Roger have made it seem that, because everyone is lying a little, to claim "A Few Extra Pounds" would mean one is actually significantly over-weight. Each justifies it to himself by blaming it on others: *If I'm the only person who falls into the category of "A Few Extra Pounds" who won't claim to be "Athletic and Toned," then potential dates will assume I'm really overweight, and I'll be stuck with only the smaller pool of those willing to date over-weight people.*

This puts honest people in a bad spot. If you insist on always telling the truth (and, worse yet, revealing all relevant information to anyone who might want to meet you), "profile inflation" will make everyone assume you are fatter, poorer, and uglier than you are. And since assertions to the contrary are still part of your uninflated profile—"I mean it, I'm not exaggerating or lying at all"—those, too, are dismissed as cheap talk. If only such people could get a Seal of Truthful-ness and form their own dating site, they would be fine. This could be one reason why Mormons and Catholics have their own dating sites, though I suspect their exclusivity is more a result of the fact that those who use these sites want to limit their search to their own group.

The Value of Being Forthcoming

But, as I noted at the very beginning of this chapter, I prominently displayed two personal features on my profile (my teenage children and the big, friendly dog who is not so familiar with the concepts of "personal space" or "hygiene") that would be big turnoffs to many people. Why did I tell the truth about those? The answer comes back to the more positive—that is, *cooperative*—side of cheap talk models. When it comes to children and dogs, my interests need to be perfectly aligned with those of potential partners. I *can't* be in a relationship with someone who will not feel comfortable with my children (they're with me half the time) or my dog (who is always with me).

This is key to cheap talk models: the more the interests of the provider and consumer of information are genuinely aligned, the more accurate the information will be. Lying—the *noncooperative* part of game theory—occurs far more often with baseline data we all share, like looks, income, and age, where everyone wants to seem as attractive as possible. But not everybody has teenagers or a big hairy sidekick, which are nonnegotiable.

In short, when the parties' interests are not completely aligned, we expect some people to misrepresent the truth. But when people's interests are aligned, lying is less of a concern.

Cheap Talk on Résumés and eBay

Two other familiar situations fit into cheap talk models: résumés and eBay ads. But there, checks on misrepresentation make these markets function far better for buyers and sellers. Few people put blatant lies on their résumés. But it is generally understood that a person's résumé will exaggerate his or her accomplishments to some degree. One recent study showed that—you guessed it—economists are prone to exaggeration on their résumés. Hiring managers understand this phenomenon and discount people's résumés accordingly.

Second, sellers of items on eBay, in hopes of drawing attention to their goods, are tempted to exaggerate the condition of their products. The quality of used goods, in terms of how well they work and how good they look, is very hard to verify over the internet.

However, these situations, unlike online dating, have built-in mechanisms to keep misrepresentation in check. References provide additional opinions to back up (or refute) a job-seeker's claims. Seller ratings on eBay, while not related to the particular product being sold, lend credibility to the overall honesty of the seller. The problem solves itself. When people know that the information they provide will be compared with information gathered elsewhere, they have more incentive to tell the truth, and others are thus more likely to believe them. Reputation and repetition almost always solve problems that would be fatal in markets where participants interact with each other only once. Like, say, online dating.

Unfortunately, online dating sites do not give us the opportunity for multiple opinions or references. Past "consumers" of the person—ex-boyfriends, ex-girlfriends, ex-spouses, even former dates—are not called on, for obvious reasons, to verify what people claim in their profiles. A few online dating sites have resorted to independent verification as an alternative way to limit lying. There is a dating site in South Korea that requires participants to submit a copy of a national registration form, diplomas, and proof of employment, which the site uses to verify age, marital history, parents' marital status, education, and type of job.

A large Chinese website (LoveMeMarryMe.com) does not go as far as the Korean site by *requiring* verification, but it does allow people to send in verification of age, education, and income. The site will also talk to a person over Skype to verify that he or she is the person in the profile picture. The largest dating site in China, Jiayuan.com, verifies customers' biographies if they submit documents. It also has a detective team that tries to identify forgeries and unearth other suspicious behavior. A British site has recently begun vetting people by cross-referencing the information they provide on Facebook and LinkedIn. That method is a less credible manner of verification, however, given that there is no guarantee that people are telling the truth on the other sites either.

The collective examples of online dating, job hunting, and eBay highlight the importance of three factors that can keep lying in check to some degree and insure that markets function smoothly. First, common preferences lead to cooperative behavior. In both the dating and job search examples, many (hopefully, most) market participants realize that a match will be a good match only if both parties prefer it to their alternatives. In the case of eBay, however, sales are zero sum—the seller's and buyer's interests are completely at odds in that the seller wants to get as much as possible for the item while the buyer wants to pay the least possible. So eBay requires a more formal process to ensure the market functions. Second, job references provide multiple opinions of a candidate's qualifications, which help minimize the degree to which job candidates can lie or exaggerate. Finally, eBay feedback mechanisms help get rid of the incentives for sellers to exaggerate the quality of the product they are selling (or to be even more aggressive in their cheating by collecting money without delivering anything). Interest in preserving one's individual reputation can mimic the types of long-term interactions that help build trust between parties whose interests are not aligned.

Cheap Talk on Television

The British game show *Golden Balls* contains my favorite example of cheap talk, in a form of cheap talk very different from the one used in the online dating world. In the final segment of the show, the two remaining contestants play a game called "Split or Steal." They are playing for a jackpot that averages well over the equivalent of $20,000 and can be more than $150,000. The game is very simple. Both contestants have two golden balls in front of them—one is marked "split" and one is marked "steal." Each contestant picks one ball and, though he knows his own choice, he does not know what the other contestant chose. When they reveal their choices, if both chose "split," they split the jackpot. If one picked "split" and the other chose "steal," the person who chose "steal" gets all the money and the person who chose "split" goes home with nothing. Finally, if both chose "steal," they *both* go home with nothing. Some well-read readers will recognize this as a modified version of the famous Prisoner's Dilemma.

What to do? You can be a nice guy and choose "split," but then you might go home empty-handed. In fact, you can never do worse for yourself by choosing "steal." Suppose the jackpot is $20,000. If the other person chooses "steal," you get nothing either way. If the other person chooses "split," you get $10,000 if you split but $20,000 if you steal. Steal is, in game theory terminology, a *dominant strategy*—it is the best thing to do no matter what the other person does.[1]

Before picking "split" or "steal," the contestants engage in a one-minute round of cheap talk; that is, they have a discussion about what they will do. Inevitably, they assure one another that they will choose the "split" ball and they implore the other person to do the same. Some of the promises and requests for cooperation are quite colorful. However, they are the essence of cheap talk. There is no reason to believe a person will split just because she says she will. In fact, about half the contestants choose "split." The cheap talk is truly cheap talk in that the contestants are no more likely to split if the other person splits than if the other person steals. That is, they play no differently based on what the other person says or does.

This game is sometimes heartbreaking but always extremely entertaining. Contestants cry and accuse each other of awful things. My favorite part is when both swear up and down that they will split and could never live with themselves if they stole, then both steal and go home with nothing.

---

1. Technically, it is a *weakly dominant strategy* because it is as good or better than the alternatives, no matter what the other person does. If the other person steals, your outcomes are equally bad no matter what you do.

They generally laugh and give each other a knowing glance that says, "Oh well, good try."

We economists love game shows because they give us an unusually clean laboratory in which to examine certain concepts, especially as they relate to game theory. Game shows, however, have one big limitation in terms of telling us much about real life—they are on television. The cheap talk in *Golden Balls* is not very useful by some measures. On the other hand, half the people choose split even though they can never do worse by stealing. Why? Some are simply good people. Even we economists can admit a few of those exist.

But the other reason to split is that so many of the people whom contestants interact with regularly will see them on the show. You might think that, relative to online dating, where their lies will at worst be exposed to their dates rather than the public, people would be reluctant to sully their reputations by openly lying on national television in hopes of tricking someone into letting them keep all the money. And yet half the people steal! The economists' view of the world and the cheapness of cheap talk is pretty powerful stuff.

Companies' Talk Is Cheap, Too

People lie or exaggerate on dating profiles, résumés, and game shows, but individuals are not the only ones who can engage in cheap talk. The logic that drives our online profiles also leads companies and their top managers to stretch the truth.

One example of corporate cheap talk was documented by Dartmouth economists Jonathan Zinman and Eric Zitzewitz, who point out that theirs is a rare case of being able to study deceptive advertising. Avid skiers search out maximum fresh powder after snowstorms, so they will often pick a mountain according to reports of how much snow fell there the day and night before. These reports are widely available on the internet. Zinman and Zitzewitz find that resorts exaggerate their snowfall, especially during periods (generally weekends) when they have more to gain by doing so.

But just as internet daters will exaggerate less if they think they will get caught, ski resorts tell the truth more when skiers can catch their lies. The proliferation of smartphones made it possible for skiers to question snow reports in real time. One SkiReport.com user post in 2009, for example, read, "Jackson Hole/Teton Village DID NOT get 15 inches today. More like 0." This immediate feedback had an effect; Zinman and Zitzewitz show that snow report exaggeration shrank noticeably at a typical resort as iPhone reception reached that resort.

Another example of corporate cheap talk is the statements made by executives. Top managers of public corporations have regular opportunities to engage in cheap talk. Consider the CEO of a large company. She is likely to own a considerable amount of stock in the company. This investment provides her with an incentive to do a good job so that the company's stock price will increase. At the same time, she wants to be sure she does not do anything that could cause her to lose her job. She also wants to try to enhance her overall reputation so that she can get other jobs, board positions, run for political office, etc. The CEO has lots of private information about the company's prospects that she can disclose or hide from the market as she sees fit.

Over the last couple of decades, there has been a rapid increase in firms' use of stock and stock options to pay CEOs, justified by the need to align the interests of CEOs and their shareholders. Sophisticated shareholders are a lot like skeptical internet daters or HR managers reading résumés. When the CEO makes a pronouncement about the prospects of the company, the stockholders know she might well be engaging in cheap talk and, as a result, they're likely to discount the CEO's statements. The CEO, knowing the market will discount what she says, really has no choice but to inflate expectations. Harvard economist Jeremy Stein analyzed the cheap talk of CEOs and how markets react, concluding that careful analysis "clearly exposes the fallacy inherent in a statement such as 'since managers can't systematically fool the market, they won't bother trying.'"

Stock analysts at investment banks, another group of prominent financial market actors, have also been widely identified as potential providers of cheap talk. When a company goes public (that is, sells its stock on a stock market), analysts at investment banks evaluate the company's prospects and make recommendations about the stock. By convention and SEC rules, the people who do these analyses are supposed to be isolated from people at the bank who handle the stock offering. However, the bank can gain overall when analysts inflate their estimates, because this makes the value of the bank's other services (especially underwriting securities) greater. In fact, if you are among those with conspiracy theory views of investment banks, there is evidence to support your suspicions. A study by Harrison Hong and Jeffrey Kubik shows that analysts who give more positive recommendations to securities underwritten by their own firms are more likely to keep their jobs.

Hsiou-wei Lin and Maureen McNichols studied in detail the recommendations of investment bank analysts at the time of new stock offerings. They compared the recommendations made by analysts at banks that underwrite a firm's securities relative to recommendations made by analysts at independent banks (those that do not underwrite a firm's securities). Lin and McNichols showed that independent analysts were considerably less generous with their forecasts than analysts whose bank had a relationship with a company. As we would expect, however, the market assumes this exaggeration. As a result, the stock market is less responsive to the recommendations made by an analyst whose bank has an underwriting relationship with the company he analyzes relative to those made by a truly independent analyst.

In addition to hanging on the words of analysts and CEOs, the stock market waits breathlessly for statements by one person in particular—the chairman of the Federal Reserve. Remember how Alan Greenspan could move the market seemingly with the mere raise of an eyebrow and how, during the financial crisis, Ben Bernanke's every word was parsed for meaning? Statements by the Fed chairman have the potential to be cheap talk. He can always say things look better or he plans to take certain actions regarding interest rates just to try to calm the markets. But the Fed is often somewhat cagey about its intentions, providing ranges—rather than exact numbers—for certain financial targets. Jeremy Stein (who has subsequently become a Federal Reserve member himself) analyzed its incentives to reveal information. He found that, if the Fed announced a precise target, such as that the inflation rate should be 2 percent, there might be situations in which it made this announcement when its true goal was 4 percent inflation. But then markets would back out the Fed's true intentions and undermine its goals.

There is less scope for manipulation when announcing a target range, such as 1–3 percent inflation. So cheap talk is more believable when a range is provided rather than when someone pins himself down with an exact figure. Perhaps, then, I should update my online profile to say that I am between forty-five and fifty-five years old and between 5 feet 8 inches and 6 feet 2 inches tall.

Cheap Political Talk

I probably don't have to work very hard to make you see that cheap talk is an important concept in another context—political campaigns. Campaign speeches are the very essence of cheap talk. Candidates can say whatever they want. But just as potential dates on Match.com discount what people say in their profiles and will not go on second dates with people who exaggerate too much, voters are skeptical of campaign promises and can use reelection to punish those who do not follow through.

Just as I've argued that economics is everywhere in online dating, economists have been infiltrating the world of political science in recent years. There has been an explosion of academic papers applying game theory ideas developed in economics to politics, including analyses of cheap talk in political campaigns.

One analysis, by Joseph Harrington, focused on how cheap a politician's campaign talk was based on how powerful the elected position was. Harrington argued that we should trust campaign promises less when the position provides the candidate with less opposition to implementing his chosen policies once elected. This finding means that mayoral candidates will be less honest in their promises than presidential candidates because the latter have to get their plans through Congress. Similarly, the president has more power over foreign policy (where there is less congressional interference) than over domestic policy, so we should expect more honesty from presidential candidates regarding domestic affairs.

Though this research means that, in general, you should trust domestic speeches by Presidential candidates more than those related to foreign policy, there are certainly exceptions. George H. W. Bush's "Read my lips: no new taxes" pledge in his Republican Presidential nomination acceptance speech is perhaps the single most famous example of political cheap talk.

Finally, it's worth noting that you should be least trusting of a candidate's statements when the electorate is more in agreement. For example, in a highly conservative area where the population is dominated by fundamentalist Christians, all politicians will claim to be anti-abortion whether that is their true opinion or not. Thinking about political promises this way helps understand the evolution of statements by such politicians as Mitt Romney and Bill Clinton, who said very different things when trying to get elected governor of states with relatively extreme political views than they said in their national presidential campaigns.

And so, hopefully, I have now convinced you of the three main points I have been trying to get across in this chapter: First, I only care about you, dear reader, learning as much economics as you possibly can—I did not write this book hoping to make any money or gain any notoriety. Second, I really am 6 feet tall, incredibly fit, and rich. And finally, if you ever happen to be playing golden balls with me, I promise I will choose "split"! Trust me.

Some Things to Take Away from Chapter 2

A Key Insight from Economics: In some situations, you have almost no choice but to lie or exaggerate about yourself because, given that other people lie and exaggerate, people are going to discount what you say.

A Valuable or Important Empirical Finding by Economists Who Study Cheap Talk: Ski resorts, on average, exaggerate when they report how much new snow they got overnight. But when the skiers can more easily verify how much new snow actually fell, exaggeration is mitigated.

When It Comes to Cheap Talk, Dating Is a Lot Like: Selling things on eBay, writing a résumé, entertaining British game shows with vaguely suggestive names.

Dating Advice: It's OK to exaggerate because everyone else does. But don't exaggerate too much or you'll be quickly dumped.

3

NETWORK EXTERNALITIES

The Facebook Effect

When I first entered the world of online dating, I was immediately drawn to Match.com. I didn't go there because it had the most attractive user interface, a unique or innovative method for matching partners, or a low price. I went there because I had heard of it and it was the biggest (or very nearly) online dating market.

That may not seem like very good logic. I don't drive a Toyota Camry, even though it is the best-selling car in America. I don't shop at Walmart, though it is the nation's biggest retailer. And I have no plans to move to China, even though it is the largest country in the world. So why did I choose Match.com rather than some cooler, niche site that would fit better with my Subaru-driving (yes, I am *that* wild) lifestyle?

I went to Match.com because by far the most important factor in a dating website's value to consumers is how many potential matches a person can find there. I wanted to be where the women were. My desire for a site used by lots of people is typical among most daters and makes it hard for new dating sites to get established. Thus, dating websites are an example of a market where demand for a product creates more demand for the product or, as economists say, the dating website is one with *network externalities*. SocialNet.com, which started in 1997 with all the makings of a successful dating site, learned about network externalities the hard way. It received $19 million from three rounds of investments from top-tier venture capital firms. It hired a top-notch management team and put a respected advertising agency to work with a $6 million budget. CEO Liz Kalodner created her own profile on the site, receiving coverage in a wide variety of media outlets. Given that one founder went on to start LinkedIn, SocialNet.com certainly had people who knew how to think about networking websites. Things looked very good. But in early 2001, SocialNet.com was sold to MatchNet at a very low price, and the SocialNet.com site was folded into other sites, the victim of daters like me who snubbed it for larger sites.

While SocialNet.com signed up customers at a fairly healthy clip, others grew even faster. Match.com was becoming the site of choice for internet daters, and the launch of eHarmony in 2000 was also very successful. This growing competition put pressure on sites like SocialNet.

Nobody Goes There Because
Nobody Goes There

Nobody was going to SocialNet because nobody was going to SocialNet. That may sound like a bad interpretation of a Yogi Berra aphorism, but it is actually a simple way of capturing the concept of a network externality—a market where demand creates demand.

The concept of *demand* is crucial in economics, and the basic idea of demand for a product is pretty straightforward. Demand goes up when a product is thought to be better because it has more features, has higher quality, or is simply more cool and hip. Demand is also typically higher when the price is lower—all else being equal, online daters will prefer a free site to one that charges a fee to join. Those two factors—price on the one hand and product features on the other—are the key drivers of demand for most products.

Products with a network externality, however, require consideration of a third feature: what are other people doing? A product has a network externality if one added user makes the product more valuable to other users. Online dating sites obviously work this way because nobody wants to be the only person on a dating site. When you stop and think about it, it's amazing any dating site ever gets started. Who signs up first? Who would join a dating site that had twenty people, much less zero or one?

Basically, an online dating site cannot succeed simply by having the features one might want, such as a great algorithm for matching people, an innovative and intuitive interface, and an interesting array of information about potential dates. If there aren't a lot of people to choose from, none of that other stuff matters.

Perhaps the easiest way to see if a product has a network externality is to think about what you look for when you choose the product. When I bought my last car, I thought about the features I wanted in a car and how much I wanted to spend. I did not think about all those Camry drivers out there and, if I had, it would have made me even less likely to buy a Camry. But when I picked an internet dating site, I thought only about where I would be most likely to find a compatible woman. The other users of the product, rather than the product itself, drove my decision. The product didn't create demand. Demand created demand.

The Facebook Effect

The rise of the internet has made network externalities more apparent and more important in many ways. As we will see, network externalities are not a new thing, but internet platforms have arisen in various applications that have made the "demand creates demand" idea especially salient. Perhaps the best example of this idea is Facebook. Essentially, the only reason anyone uses Facebook is because other people use Facebook. Each person who signs up for Facebook makes Facebook a little more valuable for everybody else. That is the entire secret of Facebook's success—it has a lot of subscribers.

That sounds like a remarkably easy business model, but of course the trick is to get the critical mass to begin with. How did the dating sites that have become large and successful get to the point where new subscribers sought them out simply because they had so many existing subscribers? In the case of Match.com, a number of things fell into place. It formed in 1993, just as the internet was becoming a significant force. It went live soon afterward, originally for free. Because it was one of the first and had a well-designed site (by the standards of the day), it signed up a few users. Then Match.com simply sat back and used its first-mover advantage because, when it had even one hundred users in a given area and other sites did not have any, it was an easy decision for a prospective dater to sign up with Match.com.

Not All Products Have Network Externalities

The idea of a first-mover advantage is regarded as important in many contexts and businesses. But there are few motivations to move first as great as a network externality. There were lots of non-dating websites that wanted to move quickly and gain first-mover advantage status in the late 1990s as the internet rose. But often the value of being first turned out to be negligible—or even negative—if others could learn from the early mover's mistakes.

Two classic examples of this phenomenon were sites seeking to become the first major online grocery store and pet-supply outlet. Webvan and Pets.com, respectively, made huge investments in establishing their brands—including airing Super Bowl ads, plastering their advertisements around major league baseball stadiums, and (in the case of the latter) developing the iconic Pets.com sock puppet. But both companies were out of business by the end of 2000. The idea of delivering pet products and groceries at home was a perfectly good business model, and Amazon has actually made very successful businesses out of both of these. There was really no advantage, however, in being the first firm into these markets, since the network externalities are limited. I don't care if my friends and neighbors use Webvan or not, so demand did not create demand.

The opposite is true in the Facebook effect described above. Facebook is a reasonably good website with a decent user interface and options. But when you get right down to it, the overwhelmingly dominant reason that so many people use Facebook is that so many people use Facebook. The demand function for a person who is picking her social network doesn't much depend on price or features, as the demand for almost all other products does. Rather, her demand for a social network is almost completely determined by which social network her friends use.

Over the last few years, Google has made one attempt after another to develop a viable alternative to Facebook. Google+, its most recent attempt, is widely touted as functionally superior to Facebook. Google+ has signed up many users, but it has not put any real dent in Facebook's dominance. Nobody is going to switch to Google+ from Facebook unless most of her friends do, too, and it seems very unlikely that whole groups of friends will act in a coordinated fashion to move from one social network to the other. Thanks to network externalities, Facebook has us right where they want us and they are probably going to keep us there.

How did Facebook get so dominant? How did it get others to switch from MySpace and other social networks?

The key is that when Facebook started and became dominant, it was focusing on users who were picking their online social networks for the first time. Facebook did not have to get most of its early adopters to switch from another site. It just had to get a group of people to agree that Facebook would be where they would network; soon those people's friends wanted to be on the same site, then so did their friends, and so on.

The Phone: Facebook before There Was Facebook

Facebook and Match.com seem like new and innovative ideas. But the idea that a product's demand can be based on a product's demand is far from new and certainly not limited to the internet. The demand for Facebook is essentially exactly the same as the demand for telephones. Why do you have a telephone? Because everybody else has one. It was a bit difficult to get people to use telephones at first. But each new user made the demand for phones a bit higher, because a phone became more valuable to everyone else. The same logic applied to fax machines when they were introduced.

Another important feature of network externalities before the internet was the shaping of standards. Have you ever stopped to think about your keyboard? Why does the top row begin with the letters Q-W-E-R-T-Y? It would be nice if the answer was that someone figured out that putting the keys where they are is the best and most efficient way to type, leading to the fastest possible typing speeds.

Of course, that's not what happened. The QWERTY keyboard was developed by two Milwaukee newspaper editors. They sold it to the E. Remington & Sons company, which made further adjustments and popularized the lay-out through its typewriter sales. One noteworthy feature of the Remington design is that it avoided putting letters that commonly follow one another (such as *t* and *h*) next to each other to prevent the arms from jamming when keys were pressed in succession. Furthermore, the letters in each row are slightly offset from the row above because the arms attached to them had to go up to the paper without hitting one another. Neither of these features is useful or relevant today, yet we all use QWERTY keyboards. Once it became a standard, everyone wanted to use the QWERTY key-board because that's just what everyone else was already doing. The QWERTY keyboard story must make Face-book executives very happy.

There are many other examples of network externali-ties like the QWERTY keyboard, where a standard took over, lasted a long time, and then demand simply created more demand. For instance, when home video recorders were just catching on back in the 1970s, the early leader was Sony's Betamax format. But when JVC introduced the VHS format, it took over before Sony could get the critical mass needed to make the network externalities work on its behalf. Similarly, in 2006–2008, the HD DVD and Blu-ray stan-dards fought for supremacy in modern videodisc technol-ogy. Toshiba retired the HD DVD in 2008 as Blu-ray took over and the HD DVD's lack of demand led to even more lack of demand.

The Value of Anonymity

Let's return to the online world and think a bit more about how network externalities work there. While many of the principles that led to Facebook's success apply to online dating sites, there are some important differences. First, while people pick Facebook because their friends are on the site, people do not pick Match.com or OkCupid because their friends are there. In fact, I would prefer that nobody I already know sees my profile on Match.com. In both cases, people join the sites because other people do, too. But people join Facebook because people they *know* join Facebook. People join Match.com because people they *don't know* join Match.com.

This creates two related reasons that explain why it is easier for a new online dating company to get some traction than it is for a new social network. First, because online daters only need a website to have a lot of people, rather than a specific set of people, they often use multiple sites. I use Match.com, OkCupid, and JDate, for example. Sure, there's a bit of setup cost involved in each site, but it's not onerous and it gives me a bigger pool of potential partners. I'm obviously not the only one who does this kind of double-dipping, given that I often see the same women on multiple sites. I only have one social network, however, because Facebook is where all my friends are.

Second, because I don't need my friends to switch from one dating site to another in order for me to do so, I'm willing to try a new dating site if it has a better product. This is why eHarmony and OkCupid were able to enter the market and flourish even though Match.com already had a successful site where demand was creating demand. eHarmony has a unique way of matching people, which it claims is more successful at helping its customers find long-term partners. It was able to get enough people to try this system that it caught on, and then the network externality led the site to mushroom. Similarly, when it debuted in 2004, OkCupid offered two things that Match.com did not have: it was free, and it had a quirky set of questions people filled out as part of setting up their profiles. These two features appealed to many people (remember, network externalities mean demand creates demand, but there can be other drivers of demand as well), especially young singles who were trying online dating for the first time. From this base, OkCupid gained enough traction for the network externalities to work their magic. But if joining OkCupid or eHarmony had only been worth it if a subscriber's friends also joined these sites (in the way that Google+ needs whole groups of friends to switch from Facebook), then I suspect neither of these two dating sites would have become successful.

Match.com = a Mall; Facebook = a Party

Network externalities work differently at Facebook and Match.com in another important way. Before I get to that, though, think briefly about the network externalities at websites such as eBay and Monster.com. These sites benefit tremendously from network externalities. But, actually, in both cases there is demand for use of these sites because there is demand from *half* the users of these sites. eBay buyers go to eBay because eBay sellers go to eBay, and eBay sellers go to eBay because eBay buyers go to eBay. Job seekers go to Monster because companies go to Monster, and companies go to Monster because job seekers go to Monster. So each new person who posts his résumé on Monster has a positive network externality for all the employers posting jobs there, but he has a negative effect on all the other job seekers because he is competing with them.

Ideally, an eBay seller would like all eBay's current buyers to shop on the site while all other sellers leave the site. Similarly, all Monster job seekers would like the companies looking for employees to stay unchanged while all the other job seekers stop using the site. Naturally, neither of those cases are going to happen. eBay buyers will look elsewhere as soon as the sellers jump ship, and firms will post elsewhere as soon as Monster job seekers leave. Facebook, on the other hand, does not work this way. The network externalities are pretty much all positive. You get the benefits of only the people you want to get the benefit of. There's no competition. Facebook is basically just a party where everyone is there to hang out and have a good time.

For heterosexual users, Match.com and other dating sites are, of course, much more like eBay than they are like Facebook in this regard. I would be delighted if half the users (the men, that is) of Match.com dropped off the site immediately, if it were not for the fact that then all the women would drop out, too. eBay and Match.com create network externalities online just the way malls and singles bars create network externalities in the physical world. Men go to singles bars because the women are there, despite the fact that other men at the bar are competing for the same women. Shoppers go to malls because the stores are there, and stores open in malls because people shop there. In each case, network externalities drive the way markets develop and congregate despite the fact that they also create competition on both sides of a market.

Same-sex dating sites seem, at first glance, to be more like Facebook—gay men go to a dating site because other gay men go to a dating site. For the most part, that pattern does indeed exist—however, unlike Facebook, each gay man who goes to a dating site is both a potential mate *and* a potential competitor. It's a very unusual market in that regard. Network externalities are critical—nobody is going to go to a gay singles dating site that has no other available men, even though it means the person has no competition. But gay men and lesbians are in the unusual and interesting position of never being able to distinguish between the future partner and the future competitor.

How We Harm Each Other by Getting in the Way

Network externalities are nice when they happen. But they are actually the exception. Usually we prefer it when other people don't want the same things we want. If Match.com (and, to an even greater extent, Facebook) are examples where demand creates demand, there are many examples where demand dampens demand. Perhaps the best example of this more traditional market is highway driving. If there were no other cars on the highway, I would probably drive a lot more than I do. I *hate* sitting in traffic. So the more drivers there are, the less I drive. Whereas Facebook is better when more people join it, highways are worse.

Economists refer to this "demand lowers demand" effect of traffic as a *congestion externality*. Unfortunately, congestion externalities are everywhere. Demand for restaurants goes down when people have to wait longer to get in. Some people who really want to go to sporting events do not buy tickets if the stadium will be crowded, parking will be difficult, and good seats are not available. That's life—if everybody wants something, it's going to be hard to get.

But there's a darker side of congestion externalities that goes back to utility functions. The following phrase rarely appears at the beginning of an interesting story, but … let's consider my evening last Saturday. One thing I have not confessed about myself is that my favorite musical artists are all female folk-country singer/songwriters. You have probably never heard of Patty Griffin, Tift Merritt, or Sarah Harmer, but I could listen to them all day. So, on this recent Saturday evening, Kathleen Edwards, who is maybe my absolute favorite artist in this obscure genre, was playing at a small nightclub in San Francisco.

I had to decide whether or not to drive up to the show. I considered (implicitly—even economists don't stop and calculate the exact utility in any given action) whether the benefits of enjoying the show were likely to be great enough to outweigh the costs of the concert financially, the cost to me in terms of time spent *not* doing other things (my son was home that evening, and we would probably have spent some quality time together), and the cost to me of the frustration of possibly sitting in traffic. In the end, I decided to go for it and I headed up to San Francisco.

Did I make the "right" decision to go? From a selfish perspective, I surely did. The concert was excellent (in case there are any Kathleen Edwards fans among my readers, "Mint" kicked ass that night) and easily outweighed the financial and hassle costs. But it may very well have been the wrong decision from a social point of view. I will admit that, when I decided whether or not to go to the concert, I never once stopped to consider that I made literally thousands of people's evening just a bit less enjoyable by going to San Francisco. For starters, I made the road a bit more crowded. I'm just responsible for one car, so I didn't have much of an effect. But I probably made several thousand people who traveled on Routes 280 and 101 get to their destination one second later than they otherwise would have. That is a cumulative cost of, let's say, one hour of people's lives that I ate up by driving to San Francisco last Saturday. Wow, I'm a jerk.

Also, I found a parking spot outside the club after driving around for at least ten minutes. When I got that parking space, some other poor guy didn't get it and spent more time looking for his spot. When he finally got his spot, he kept a woman who was right behind from getting hers, and so on. Wow, I'm a bigger jerk!

Finally, the concert was the kind where everyone stood up and crowded in toward the stage. Because I was there, lots of other people at the show stood just a tiny bit further from the stage and, as a result, enjoyed the show a tiny bit less. Unsurprisingly, I am a jerk yet again!

I suddenly feel like crap about going to San Francisco last Saturday night. I sucked a lot of utility away from a bunch of other people.

I'm not a bad person, and neither are you—even though neither of us *ever* considers, when making some decisions, that we are lowering other people's utility. Unless you are in denial about global warming, you probably at least think about the externality you are generating when you drive your car or create carbon in another way. Priuses and plug-in electric cars are selling at a brisk pace these days, suggesting that lots of people feel bad about their carbon externality. But why don't they feel bad about their congestion externalities? Why don't any of those same people change their habits so they don't get in my way when I drive to the next concert?

When it comes right down to it, we are selfish. With a few exceptions, we do not consider other people's utility when we make decisions. That's fine in many cases, but not when there are congestion externalities. You may have heard proposals for a "carbon tax" or emissions restrictions designed to manage the pollution externality of driving and other emissions. But you rarely see an attempt to manage congestion externalities—to get people to "internalize" the costs they impose on others by making the roads more crowded.

There are a few examples of such controls, though. The most prominent is the sizable charge imposed on people who drive into an area of central London known as the Congestion Charging Zone. Vehicles driving in this area on weekdays must pay a fee of up to £10 (over $15) per day. When the system was introduced in 2003, it cut traffic in the area by approximately 40 percent and increased traffic speeds by about one third (though that only meant reaching an average of 11 miles per hour). Over time, traffic returned to the same levels as before the charges were first instituted, but the congestion may well have been even greater without the charges.

Other attempts to manage congestion externalities have been less successful. As anyone who has driven in New York knows, traffic there is terrible on a typical workday. A proposal by then-mayor Michael Bloomberg to tax people driving in the city was never implemented. Modeled on the London plan, Bloomberg's plan would have charged cars $8 on any weekday that they drove in Lower Manhattan. While the plan had a great deal of support, it was killed by groups that thought it was regressive (that is, fees would fall disproportionately on poor and middle-class drivers) or would lead to increased traffic in areas near, but outside, the zone.

Los Angeles freeway traffic is legendary. The highways in Southern California can be like parking lots at almost all hours of the day. Yet there have been few serious attempts to get individuals to take their contributions to these conditions into account when deciding whether or not to drive.

Not all negative externalities are congestion externalities. Congestion externalities lead one person to lower another person's utility because the first person's use of a certain product makes the second person's demand for (or enjoyment of) that product lower. Carbon externalities are simpler—when I drive, I cause pollution, which hurts you whether you drive or not. Lots of externalities work this way. People take some action and it hurts lots of other people, no matter what those other people arc doing.

In theory, we can fix externalities with taxes and other limits on people's actions. But it can be very difficult to get the government to take the necessary action because often the group that causes an externality is well organized and vocal while the victims of the externality are diffuse, such that the individual victims suffer so little they can't be bothered to do much about the problem.

The Good Side of Externalities

By now it should be clear that the network externalities (the "demand creates demand" effect) of online dating are just one of several types of externalities. There are congestion externalities, such as driving, where demand lowers demand. There are more general negative externalities, such as polluting, where one person's actions hurt other people directly (rather than making something both people consume less valuable). So that leaves us with only the best kind of externality left to talk about—*general positive externalities*.

Each additional woman who joins Match.com increases my utility because there is some chance I will meet her and we will hit it off. But that same woman (or some man or child, for that matter) can do other things that, even though we don't really interact, increase my utility. For example, I have a neighbor who is a very good gardener and I have a view of his house from my house. He is happy to have such a nice garden, since he gets to see it every day. But it is also good for me, given that I also see it regularly. His lawn increases my utility. He should charge me some of the cost of keeping his lawn looking nice because I am happier as a result. Many housing associations, in effect, do this. They take actions such as instituting rules that ensure that all the homeowners will keep their lawns looking nice. In the absence of such a rule, many homeowners would underinvest in lawn maintenance. But when all the residents are obligated to keep their lawns looking nice, the positive externalities (which can come in the form of daily enjoyment and higher property values) are maximized.

Positive externalities are a primary motivation for public education systems (fairness, of course, is another). People have a great deal of incentive to invest in education. As I will discuss in chapter 9, more education generates lots of benefits for the person who gets it. Education leads to higher income and job-related benefits, more enjoyable and less monotonous work, better health, and other good things. But if a person is educated, her neighbors also benefit (on average). For example, she likely pays more taxes, receives fewer transfers from the government, and is much less likely to engage in criminal activity. So her neighbors have to pay less in taxes and they feel a bit safer.

In places where there are no public schools, children (and their parents) often must decide whether to spend the considerable sum it costs to go to a private school. Imagine a little girl without access to public school who thinks that going to a paid school is pretty close to worth the money but not quite. Though it would be quite inconvenient, she could go door-to-door in her neighborhood and ask for contributions to her school fund. She could remind each person that an education would make her less of a burden on their taxes in the future and less likely to mug them. Maybe she would collect enough to go ahead and enroll.

Luckily, aspiring students do not have to go door-to-door if they live in just about any developed country. In the United States, children can simply enroll in the local public school. As a society, we have decided that the best way to get children to produce the positive externalities of an education is to just provide the education for them. In fact, we have gone one step further and insisted that children go to school at least until they turn sixteen (in most places). Many kids drop out at that point, and some become the type of people who mug other people regularly, but the odds of that happening are much lower than if they never went to school. If we could just figure out how to make sure the school also teaches children to take their effect on traffic into account when they decide whether to drive or not, the investment in education would be even better. But who learns anything in schools these days? All the kids are too busy on Facebook.

Some Things to Take Away from Chapter 3

A Key Insight from Economics: Being the first to offer a product in a market where demand creates demand can lead to one of the most powerful barriers to entry a company can have.

A Valuable or Important Empirical Finding by Economists Who Study Network Externalities: In an ideal world, the government could do a lot of things that would make the world a better place, including charging more to drive on the highway, to emit carbon, and to drive in New York City during the day.

When It Comes to Network Externalities, Dating Is a Lot Like: Social networking, online auctions, going to the mall.

Dating Advice: Pick a big online dating site. This is a time to be a follower, not a leader.

4

SIGNALING

Putting Your Money Where Your Mouth Is

An online dating site in Korea recently ran a special event over a nine-day period that was sort of a cross between online dating and speed dating. Participants browsed online profiles as in standard online dating; over a five-day proposal period, they could show up to ten people on the site that they were interested in a date with them. In addition, during that period some participants could offer a virtual rose along with two of their date requests. This, in effect, told the recipient that he or she was among the highest choices of the person offering the rose. Next, there was a four-day period during which people responded (essentially yes or no) to the proposals they received. The company then matched up the mutually inter-ested pairs.

Participants paid the equivalent of about $50 to participate in this event, which is a little less than the one-month fee for this particular dating site's standard service (essentially the Korean equivalent of Match.com).

Why did the site add the element of the virtual rose, and did it affect the outcomes of the dating arrangements? The answers are that a couple of economists talked them into it and yes, it had large effects. The idea of *signaling* something to someone you are trying to impress was modeled by Michael Spence in the early 1970s (and won Spence a Nobel Prize in 2001), and these economists wanted to try it out.

Signaling picks up where we left off in chapter 2. Suppose I go on an online dating site and send a message to a woman in which I say, "You have the most attractive and interesting profile of any woman I've seen on this site in the last year." That is cheap talk. I could say that to everyone I message. The woman who gets this kind of message has no reason to believe me. In fact, the saying "I bet you say that to all the girls" has been a staple of songs, TV, and movies for decades. So, suppose I want to show (signal) that I really, *really* mean it when I say the profile is the best I've seen in a while. How can I do that? I need to find a way to prove it—to put my money where my mouth is, as it were.

In their promotion, the Korean website did just this for participants. These online daters got two free "I really mean it" opportunities that were completely credible. If I got a rose in an experiment like that, I would know that the person who sent it had chosen me over all the other profiles (or at least all but one)! That's very flattering and would surely make me more likely to respond favorably. But note that what makes the signal work in this case is that it *costs something*.

Participants have to give up something very important—the ability to show special interest in others—when they use the virtual rose. That's the key to signaling, and it's what elevates talk from cheap to credible. Signals become meaningful only if they are costly.

It's very hard to use signaling in standard online dating to get a first date. There's not much you can do credibly to signal interest. Everything is cheap talk. But signaling can begin in earnest with the first date. We know that women, for example, are attracted to men who make more money (see chapter 9). All claims of making a lot of money in an online profile are cheap talk and therefore not credible. You can say you make a $1 million a year, and you can even post pictures of yourself in settings that suggest wealth. Given that nobody verifies your income and thanks to the wonders of Photoshop, there is no way to tell if your profile is accurate. But on the first date, you get your chance to show your wealth. You can take her to fancy places and pick up the bill, you can wear expensive clothes, and you can make sure your date sees you drive up in your BMW. (Even though I'm writing about it, I'm not very good at this technique—I usually suggest first dates at a coffee shop, I wear jeans, and I drive a Subaru.)

Of course, people can fake it through the first date or two—that is, spend above their means—but it's costly to do so. That cost is what leads to *separation*—the ability to tell the real rich guys from the fakes. Only the guys who really do make a lot of money can keep on making the large expenditures needed to impress a woman with their income and so, after a few dates, the claim becomes credible.

Education as a Signal

When Michael Spence originally explained the idea of signaling, online dating had not yet been invented and he had to think of another way to convey the concept. He imagined a world where education serves no productive use whatsoever. Colleges exist only so that prospective employers can figure out which people they want. So imagine there are exactly two types of people in the world—those who are talented and those who are innately unskilled. Each person knows which type he is, but talented individuals cannot simply tell people "I'm talented" because, as we saw in chapter 2, such cheap talk proves nothing. Employers need to know, though, who the talented people are so that they can put them in the higher-level jobs.

How can employers figure out who's who? Suppose that only the talented people will be able to graduate from college. The unskilled can go to college if they want, but the coursework will be too taxing and they will end up dropping out before they finish. Knowing that they are unskilled, these people simply bypass college and accept a lower-level job. But the talented people can prove their skill level by graduating from college. They may learn nothing useful in college, but they show employers that they are talented and, as a result, they are eligible for higher-level jobs.

Education has solved our cheap talk problem. A potential employee puts his money where his mouth is by spending a lot of time and money on his education to prove (rather than just say) that he is talented. But this system will work only under two very important conditions. First, it must be that only the talented people can make it through college. If the untalented people can also graduate from college, they will go to college and be able to claim they are talented. Second, it has to be the case that a college degree is actually a useful indicator of the person's talent in the job market. If only some people can get through college, but those people are not necessarily the ones who will be good employees, then the system breaks down.

A recent meeting I had with the owner and CEO of a Midwestern cement block company shows that at least some people believe in the signaling explanation of the value of education. In explaining why he hires college-educated people for certain positions, he told me, "It doesn't mean you're smarter by having a college degree. It means you've put up with a lot of stuff for four years and you were able to get through it." I suspect this CEO has never heard of Michael Spence, but his explanation of signaling would have made Spence proud. Hopefully, the signaling idea does not fully explain why colleges exist—as a teacher, I sure like to think people actually learn something in school. But signaling may explain some of the value of going to college (or graduate school or even trade school).

Just as the cement block company CEO had an intuitive feel for signaling in education, another unexpected but very clever interpretation of signaling can be found in the comic writer David Sedaris's description of the immigration process. In a *New Yorker* essay, Sedaris first bemoans the fact that, every few years, he and his partner have to renew the visas that allow them to live in the United Kingdom: "This involved going to the dismal town of Croydon and spending a day in what was always the longest and most desperate line I had ever imagined." While most people in such a situation would see this process as a cruel injustice or proof that government operations are always inefficient, Sedaris went on to point out that the British government may have been trying to implement signaling. "People think it's easy to leave home and resettle in another country, but in fact it's exhausting, and purposely so. The government hopes to weed out the lazy."

Whether it is relevant to education and immigration or not, the signaling idea applies quite nicely to the virtual rose. Think of someone on the dating site as a potential employee who wants to show potential dates that he is talented—which, in this case, means he is *especially* interested in her relative to other women on the site. If he writes her a note to that effect, it will look just like the notes she gets from less interested (less talented) potential dates. So he has to do something very costly (using his precious virtual rose) to convince her.

Does Signaling Work?

So did signaling work? Did the virtual roses have any effect? In fact, they worked tremendously. If a man or woman sent a proposal, the recipient accepted about 15 percent of the time. But about 18 percent of proposals that came with a virtual rose were accepted, which means sending a rose increased the chances of acceptance by about one fifth. Would writing "I really want to meet you" have worked so well? Probably not, since participants can say that to anyone.

Looking at who accepted which proposals provides more evidence for the importance of virtual roses as a means of making a credible proposal. Specifically, the company that runs the dating site is able to quantify the likely desirability of any given participant. Tracking height, earnings, education, and other characteristics, the firm can use past results to determine which participants will be viewed as more or less desirable. The virtual roses do not matter that much for the most desirable people. That's no great surprise—those people already expect to be among the most sought after. But the less desirable people are much more responsive to roses. To them, being told somebody really wants to meet them might seem like cheap talk.

It turns out that the effect of a virtual rose is largest on the middle desirability group. They are almost twice as likely to accept a proposal with a rose than one without. To them, being told in a credible manner that they really are particularly attractive is very meaningful. They have heard a lot of cheap talk in their lives and they value someone backing it up. Or, put another way, the rose is a meaningful *investment* in the person because the sender had to give up other opportunities in order to send it.

It would be very interesting to be able to follow the rose send-ers and recipients to see if they led to more long-term happy relationships. But we will have to settle for hoping for the best.

How to Show Someone "I *Really* Want This Job"

The job market does not have virtual roses, and that can be a problem for some people. The inability to signal on the job market can be especially problematic for people who are over-qualified for jobs that, for some reason, they really want.

Consider Bob, a graduate student who is about to receive his degree from a top business school and would appear to have lots of great options at his disposal. He has already had a few years of success at a top investment bank and has an offer to return to the New York office with a very attractive compensation policy. But Bob is married to Cindy, who grew up in Cincinnati. They have decided that they would prefer to move to Cincinnati, live in a nice house near Cindy's parents, and both take jobs that are rewarding yet not *too* intense. They both want to have time to spend with their children, helping out at school and coaching soccer, and, of course, have some spare time to read economics books. (Up until the book part, this was based on a couple I actually know.)

Bob sends his résumé and a cover letter to numerous Cincinnati firms of various sizes and in a wide range of industries. He thinks (and, in fact, he is correct) that just about any of these firms would be very lucky to have a young manager who could help the company grow and/or implement more professional practices. But he is disappointed to find that these firms do not respond to his inquiries and show no interest in hiring him.

What's the matter? These firms are exactly the same as the Korean online daters in the middle-desirability group. They have limited resources, so why bother with someone who appears to be out of their league? They would like to hire Bob, but people like Bob don't work for companies like them. If he means it, he's going to have to do something to show them he means it.

Bob is in a tricky position. He's already tried cheap talk, and it failed—his cover letter explained how much he wants to move to Cincinnati and work for these companies. He needs to take more drastic action. He needs to do something that has two qualities of an effective signal (remember these qualities, as we will revisit them throughout this chapter): he needs to take an action that is *costly* to himself and that is *easier or more valuable* for him than for someone who does not have the qualities the signal receiver is looking for (which, in this case, is a strong desire to work for the companies).

Unfortunately, it is very difficult to come up with a signal that meets Bob's needs. He could offer something truly dramatic—such as taking no salary for a while. But that might appear so unusual or desperate that it would backfire. Alternatively, he could buy one of these companies—with his connections from business school and his past work as an investment banker, he could probably pull it off. But then he would own a company and probably not be in a position to spend the quality time with his family that he is looking for.

One thing he could do that might work is spend a lot of time researching the specific needs of a few of the potential employers and send them a detailed plan for how his skills would help them address their problems or opportunities. That strategy would be both costly to him and, assuming he did a good job identifying their needs, would be something only someone who is the right type for the firm could do. So it would have the features of a good signal. But it would also be a risky strategy and, because it's so unusual, might simply seem weird.

A group of economists took this idea seriously and figured out how to make sending an "I *really* want this job" signal credible (and not weird). Unfortunately, they are so far limited to a small set of employees—other economists. Every fall, people who are in the last year of an economics PhD program apply for positions at universities, government agencies, and other employers. They send a set of materials to each place they would like to apply, and their advisers send reference letters to those places on the applicants' behalf. At the same time, economists make contacts with their connections throughout the economist network, either "selling" their students or asking for input on which students to hire. A pecking order develops where some applicants are deemed worthy of consideration at the very top institutions, others at the second tier, and so on.

This system works reasonably well, but there has, historically, been one problem. The "Bob from Cincinnati" economists have had trouble convincing the second- or third-tier schools that they really would like to work there and that, even if offered a faculty position at Harvard, they would prefer a less prestigious position (for geographic, lifestyle, or other reasons). Since this is the one job market where anyone might listen to the advice of a bunch of economists, several of them got together and proposed a solution. They suggested that the American Economic Association (AEA) set up a system whereby each person applying for a new job as an economist could send up to two private signals to potential employers. That is, they allowed each job seeker to send two virtual roses (though they used different terminology since, in this context, calling it a rose would be a bit strange).

The AEA specifically advises applicants *not* to use their two precious signals for their top two choices but rather suggests sending them to employers "you like but that might otherwise doubt whether they are likely to be able to hire you." They also advise applicants not to waste signals on top-tier employers that virtually everyone looking for a job is interested in.

These signals have largely been used in the way they were intended. Students at top-tier schools used them to signal geographic preferences and specific interest in second-tier employers. Institutions looking for employees took the signal very seriously—sending a signal increased a candidate's probability of getting an interview from about 25 percent to about 32 percent. The effects were much bigger for applicants to liberal arts colleges because jobs at such institutions are not as attractive to the typical economist; there is a substantial subset of economists who like the teaching and small-class orientation of liberal arts colleges, though, and the signal is a very valuable way for them to show these schools they *really* want a job there.

The success of signaling on the economics job market (and, less directly, on Korean internet dating sites) suggests other employers may be able to use signaling to sort through applicants. In recent years, Google has gotten as many as seventy-five thousand job applicants in a given week—obviously, that is a lot of résumés to filter through. Undoubtedly, many (probably most) of those applicants know little about Google other than that they make cool products and have a reputation for being a good place to work. Some may apply just because of the well-known free and high-quality food in Google's cafeterias. How can Google save itself the trouble of sorting through all those résumés and get people to apply to Google only if it is the case that they would be a good fit and are qualified? That is, can Google get applicants to include the equivalent of a virtual rose?

Remembering our two conditions for an effective signal, a signaling system at Google would involve creating a signal that is costly and that only the most promising applicants would bother with. It also has to be the case that the relatively promising applicants can figure out who they are and the unpromising applicants can realize they should not apply. Google has experimented with a few methods along these lines, including posting brainteasers on highway billboards in Silicon Valley. This ploy encourages those who can answer the brainteaser, who are presumably the same people who would be good Googlers (they really are called that), to apply for a job. But the billboards alone are clearly not discouraging the bad fits from applying, given the high volume of applications.

One thing companies like Google can do is simply charge a fee for sending in an application. That probably would offend a lot of people at first and would certainly go against conventional norms of employer behavior. But what if Google charged a person $10 to submit a résumé for consideration and sent the money to a charity? That might well serve the company's purpose of cutting down the résumé traffic while creating a public relations advantage. Google would be able to say that its hiring process led to millions of dollars per year in charitable donations.

Google may not need to worry too much about signaling anyway, given that it gets a lot of marketing value out of its recruiting process. But there are lots of other companies that are more like the medium-attractive Korean daters or the liberal arts colleges trying to hire economists. They can go looking for employees on Monster.com or the like, but how do they know which ones would be good fits and would be serious about taking a job at the company? It's hard for the company to do much to make people signal, but Monster. com could easily mimic the economist market signal process. Monster could give all people who post their résumé online one "Favored Employer" credit each month. Then the job applicant could, once a month, send this signal to one potential employer to credibly show that the company is at the top of his list.

This signal would, if all went according to my plan, be good for everyone. It would allow some people to move to better jobs. And it would enable some firms to hire people who have carefully thought through their options and truly want to work for them.

The Common Application Ruins Signaling . . .

While the online dating market is constantly playing out in real time, the college application process is slower and more regimented. Once a year, colleges and high school seniors go through a matching ritual that is, at least by the way some people act, more important than the hunt for life partners on dating sites. But while virtual roses may be useful in dating and could potentially be useful for Google and other employers, colleges and universities can ask people to expend a traditional costly signal—real money in the form of an application fee.

Application fees are standard for college and graduate school applicants, often making the admissions office a profit center for the university. These fees presumably provide some signaling value for these schools—applicants typically give some thought to their chances of admission and are reluctant to spend $75 on a sure rejection. But, given the very low acceptance rate at many selective schools, these fees are not high enough to dissuade all unlikely candidates (and, given the fairly random nature of the admissions process, we would expect a lot of people to apply hoping to get lucky).

In addition to the fees charged by schools, there are other costs to sending an application, including getting references, writing essays, and filling out paperwork. The Common Application system, which was introduced by fifteen colleges in 1975 but did not become widespread until quite recently, aims to make college applications more efficient. The Common Application organization seeks to promote "equity" and "access." Anyone who has applied to college will immediately see the value in the Common Application (or the Common App, as it is widely known), as it means applicants submit much of the required material only once rather than entering all the data and information for each school to which they apply.

But the Common App is the *anti-signal*. It may actually make the application process *less* efficient. How can saving all college applicants lots of time and effort be inefficient? Maybe the Common App has made applying to college too easy. If there are important differences between colleges, then it probably makes sense for students to carefully think through which colleges best fit their interests and focus their application efforts on those schools. The old system did that—students made much more of an investment in each school they applied to. The system had the two things we look for in a good signaling system. It was costly to the applicant to signal (that is, apply) and, assuming students could figure out which schools they would like best, the signal really did mean (in general) that the person was qualified. Applying to a given school revealed more private information about students' interest in the school than it does now, when they can just hit a few more computer keys and apply to another college.

The downside of the system was highlighted recently when the University of Chicago became one of the last elite schools to consider adopting the Common App. In protesting the move to the Common App, one student wrote, "I cannot express how much the Uncommon Application [University of Chicago's specific application] meant to me during the soul-destroying ordeal of the college application process." One analyst covering the University of Chicago said colleges should be trying to find "unique" students and "good matches." That is, they should try to elicit more signals in the application process. The University of Chicago eventually adopted the Common App, though the school requires a supplement in which students address quirky essay questions that (theoretically) reveal their interest and fit with the school.

Another great example of an anti-signal in the modern world is birthday wishes on Facebook. In the old days, keeping track of your friends' birthdays and sending them birthday wishes (in the form of a card or, at the least, an e-mail) took some effort. But Facebook ruined that. I used to get a weekly e-mail telling me which of my Facebook friends had a birthday that week. Now I've taken it a step further—my iPhone lists these birthdays on my daily calendar. So, when I see it is someone's birthday, I can quickly get on Facebook and write "Happy Birthday" or the like on his or her wall. I guess it's nice to get birthday wishes from a lot of people, but I don't like this new system. Knowing that each person spent an average of fifteen seconds wishing me a happy birthday takes all the fun out of it. More than one person has put a birthday wish on my Facebook page consisting entirely of "hb." Two lowercase letters! I hate to be anachronistic, but I like the old days when kids had to write separate essays for each college and people had to work a little to wish each other happy birthday.

. . . but Early Applications Are a Great Signal

These days, the main signaling mechanism available to college applicants is early admission. Most elite schools use a process whereby an applicant can apply to only one school for early admission. This system is essentially identical to the virtual rose in the Korean dating site's event or the economists' job market signal. Because the student can apply to only one school for early admission, it is a credible way to say, "This is *the* school I really want to go to." On the positive side, that tells the school the student is relatively likely to be a good fit. On the more cynical side, it helps the school increase its "yield" (the fraction of accepted applicants that choose to attend) and, therefore, how *U.S. News and World Report* and others rank the school.

Whichever of these interpretations you prefer, there's no doubt that colleges interpret the signal of an early application quite positively. A recent study by Chris Avery and Jonathan Levin showed that admission rates to the most elite colleges were twice as high during the early admissions process as they were during the regular admission cycle. Some of the findings can be explained by the fact that the most qualified students were more likely to apply early to these schools. But, for a given student (that is, holding test scores, GPA, and the like constant), there was still a substantial increase in probability of acceptance by applying early. Across the schools Avery and Levin analyzed—which were all highly selective schools, including most Ivy League universities, other top universities, and elite liberal arts colleges such as Williams College—applying early increased an applicant's chances by approximately 20 to 30 percent. An early applicant was about as likely to be accepted as a regular applicant who scored 100 points higher on the SAT exam. Avery and Levin point out some potential weaknesses of early admission, such as that it forces schools and students to make decisions earlier than might be ideal. But they show clearly that signaling is important in the admissions process.

Signaling Can Work for High School Dropouts, Too

The admissions process at Ivy League schools may be interesting, but it isn't all that relevant to the population at large. But don't worry—signaling in education is not just for top colleges. At the other end of the academic spectrum, high school dropouts may want to do some signaling, as well. Consider the real-life case of Mildred. At fifteen, as she now reminisces, she "knew it all" and "could do it all" and dropped out. A few years later, she had a baby and wanted to provide him with good opportunities. High school dropouts do not have great career options. In 2005, the average high school dropout earned $17,000 per year, while high school graduates who did not go to college earned $27,000—about 50 percent more. Mildred wanted to move up in the world, so she did the only thing a high school dropout can do—she worked towards a General Equivalency Diploma (GED), which allowed her to apply for jobs available only to high school graduates.

Though not all GED earners are as ambitious, Mildred actually took the process much further, going on to college and graduate school. She is now a Health Administrator for the Texas Department of Criminal Justice, earning a healthy living. What made that career possible? The signal of a GED.

The holder of a GED, unlike other high school dropouts, has passed a test showing that she is educationally equivalent to a high school graduate. The test shows potential employers two things. First, it indicates that the person has the literacy and numeracy, as well as the understanding of science and social studies, that one would expect of a high school graduate. For many jobs, this aptitude is an important indicator that the person has the skills required. This part is not a signal as it has been described so far in this chapter because the skills are directly useful, not just a cost incurred strictly to separate GED holders from others.

The second thing the test indicates is that the person had the initiative to take it and, if necessary, study whatever she needed to learn to pass it. The direct and indirect costs of taking the GED exam are not trivial. The test itself lasts approximately eight hours and requires the person to find a test center, complete forms, and take the test during certain hours on certain days. There are also fees, which vary by state. In Texas, for example, where Mildred took the exam, the test currently costs approximately $100 and another $20 to retake any parts the person fails. That is not a great deal of money, but it is far from trivial for many high school dropouts. In addition, the typical person who takes the GED exam studies for twenty hours or more. The time invested, plus the cost of practice classes, adds considerable expense.

It is this second part that is often thought to be a *costly signal* to employers. There are probably a lot of high school dropouts who could pass the GED exam but do not bother to go through the effort and cost. If colleges and employers of high school graduates prize initiative and ambition, then the GED has both properties of a useful signal. It's costly, given the time and money required. And those who are willing to make the investment are more valuable to employers and colleges than those who do not make the investment.

That sounds logical, perhaps, but remember that having a GED might also just mean the person actually knows more than someone without a GED. Economists John Tyler (not the tenth president), Richard Murnane, and John Willett figured out a way to distinguish between the "GED holders have better skills" and "GED is a valuable costly signal" ideas. They looked at how much more money GED holders made relative to other high school dropouts in a number of states that had different passing scores for the GED tests. That setup allowed them to look at equally capable people who had all done the work to prepare for the GED, but some of whom had failed the test because of the state they lived in.

Tyler and his coauthors found some striking results. Signaling matters a lot for young white dropouts. The signal value of a GED increases their earnings by almost 20 percent. But there is no evidence that the signal does anything for minorities. While that may at first glance seem puzzling, there are some pretty good potential explanations. It turns out that many minorities who earn a GED are in prison, while the fraction of GED-holding whites who are convicts is much lower. So it could be that there is a second, unintended, signal sent by minorities earning a GED: "There's a pretty good chance I'm in jail."

Burn a Big Pile of Money on the First Date

GEDs, signaling at Google, and the economist job market signals are nice examples of how the basic principles behind the Korean dating site's virtual roses apply to other situations. But now let's return to the other dating example I mentioned—showing off on the first date. We know that men are, on average and holding everything else constant, much more likely to get a response on a dating site if they claim to make more money. But they have to back up that cheap talk by somehow showing their date they really do have a lot of money.

Let's imagine a man named Phillip who is looking for a relationship. On his Match.com profile, among his many positive attributes, Phillip lists a healthy income. Phillip has a first date with Natalie and he wants to make sure she believes he actually has a lot of money. Upon meeting him, Natalie is pretty quickly able to determine that Phillip is as tall as he claimed to be and that his online profile pictures accurately depicted his attractiveness. But she still suspects that Phillip is not as rich as he claimed to be and that he is just saying he has money to try to get her into bed. How can Phillip dispel this notion? (At least, how can he dispel the part about not being rich? I don't have a lot of insight on the "getting her into bed" part.)

One Chinese adviser of young women looking for a husband essentially recommends eliciting signals both of interest and of wealth. She says to make the man do the traveling on the first date. She also says to closely examine his watch, cell phone, belt, and shoes and to be suspicious of a man who keeps the receipt.

Even if Natalie is following this advice, Phillip can take things a step further and show her his recent tax returns as evidence of his wealth. But that would be rather weird behavior, thereby signaling something less positive than he is aiming for. One thing that would certainly be an effective signal, but again bring his psychological well-being into question, is to light some money on fire when he meets Natalie. Weird? Yes. But a very effective signal—it is costly, but far less so for people who actually have the qualification he's trying to signal. So Natalie would probably think he really is rich. Depending on her taste for eccentricity, secondhand smoke, and public spectacles, it may or may not work. If Phillip wanted a more environmentally friendly (but still rather odd) way of doing the same thing, he might write a check to a charity of Natalie's choice when he meets her.

Money burning in the literal sense is very rarely seen in practice. The Joker burns a big pile of money in one of the Batman movies, *The Dark Knight*, to prove to his mafia coconspirators that his goals are broader than just making money. While that display is an extremely successful signal in the movie, it's not very realistic in a literal sense. But people and firms burn money figuratively on a regular basis for the signaling value of doing so. One example is some forms of advertising. A lot of advertising conveys literally no information about a product. Firms just spend a lot of money to generate a positive image among customers. But one way to look at this practice is that the firms are, in essence, saying, "We have a great product and we are going to waste a lot of money bringing that fact to your attention. But we know this will pay off because, since our product is so great, we know you will keep using it and make our investment pay off." Or, put more succinctly, firms are signaling. They are wasting money on advertising, but the value of the signal is higher for the better products and firms. If a firm spends a great deal of time advertising an inferior product, it may get people to try the product, but repeat business will be slow, and negative word of mouth will discourage future shoppers.

The signaling justification for advertising will work only if companies expect customers to have long-term relationships with the product or expect satisfied customers to spread the word to other customers. Advertising in tourist areas, where the customers are more transient, might be effective in the more traditional sense. But it would not convey a useful signal because low-quality firms have just as much to gain from advertising as high-quality firms. Advertising can be a useful signal of quality only when high-quality firms can expect ads to generate a steady stream of income that low-quality firms cannot expect. For example, advertising of cars and food items that will be purchased repeatedly is likely at least partially driven by an attempt to signal the difference between high- and low-quality goods.

A much more direct way to signal quality to customers is a warranty. Unlike advertising, this device is not simply burning money. It is promising to burn money if the firm's product is not high quality. Warranties have both qualities of a good signal—they are costly, and that cost is lower for the high-quality parties that are trying to signal. Think of two car manufacturers—Honda, which has a reputation for reliable cars, and Jaguar, which produces cars that are very attractive but are notorious for being in the repair shop frequently. Honda would find it much less expensive to offer a generous warranty on its cars than Jaguar, given the lower costs it would likely face as a result. Jaguar could try to change its reputation by offering a long and comprehensive warranty, but (if its reputation is justified) the company would find it too expensive to do so.

Of course, one big limitation of warranties is that they are of no use if there is a chance the provider will go out of business. A warranty becomes mere cheap talk if the firm may not be able to honor it because the signal ends up having lower costs for the low-quality firms.

Burning Money at the IPO

Just as there are a lot of great guys on Match.com, there are a lot of young upstart companies with great new technologies. However, just as there are also a lot of liars and cads on

Match.com, there are also a lot of young upstart companies with stupid ideas and products that will never work properly. So an investor hoping to put some money into the technology sector faces the same problem as a woman perusing Match.com—who is the special one and who is the loser?

That question vexes venture capitalists, bankers, and other investors on a daily basis. Investors have a lot of ways to find clues that online daters do not have access to—disclosures, news items, and rumor blogs provide some inside scoop. At the same time, managers of the firms that truly have good ideas and good prospects are looking to make their potential clear to everybody else just as our friend Phillip was trying to make it clear to Natalie that he really does have a lot of money. How can the managers of a company put their money where their mouth is and show the world that they are worth investing in?

One possible answer is that they can burn money (or, more accurately, give it away) when the firm sells stock to the public. Think about two companies that look exactly the same when they are about to sell stock to investors for the first time. They each want to raise as much money as they can in the process, and the managers of each firm know exactly how good their firm's prospects are. One CEO knows that her firm is on its way to being the next Google, while the other knows her firm will be moderately successful. The CEO whose firm has excellent prospects has an incentive to underprice her company—to sell it for too little. By doing so, she shows investors her quality (and the firm's quality), which will pay off when she needs to raise money again in the future. If she never expects to raise more money, signaling quality by selling stock for too little would be a waste.

On the other hand, the CEO who knows her firm will only be moderately successful will not underprice the stock when she sells it. It is too costly to signal quality because her firm will not be going back to the market to raise more money at a time when it looks much better. She wants to get as much as she possibly can for her stock now because she knows she is not likely to get a much better offer later.

LinkedIn offered stock to public shareholders for the first time in 2011. On the day the shares were offered, they doubled in value. Such immediate growth means that the company sold these shares for about half as much as they could have commanded. The investors who bought LinkedIn shares at $45 when the market opened on May 19, 2011, could have sold those shares for over $90 by the end of the day. *New York Times* columnist Joe Nocera said LinkedIn was "scammed by its bankers" for selling at such a low price. But others have argued that LinkedIn was simply signaling its quality and hopes to later reap the benefits when it sells even more stock at a higher price. Andrew Ross Sorkin, another *Times* reporter and columnist, explained this strategy a few days later, writing, "LinkedIn only sold a fraction of the company, a little more than 5 percent. So if the stock price happens to hold up, the company will be able to raise a lot more cash. That is what the company's management actually cares about."

Zynga, a social gaming company, had a less happy fate. On its first day of trading, the stock actually fell in value. The managers and bankers left no money on the table, apparently, feeling no need to signal about its future prospects. While factors other than signaling affect stock prices when firms sell shares to the public, these two examples would lead one to predict a brighter future for LinkedIn than for Zynga.

Now, I'm not saying Zynga should have purposely given away a lot of money on the first day it sold stock, but shareholders may be able to learn something from the fact that Zynga didn't leave money on the table for future stock offerings. More generally, I don't advocate burning a pile of money in any situation. It's a big waste of good money, and who needs more pollution? But metaphorically burning money in the job market, the stock market, the college application process, and of course when dating is a great way to show you really mean what you say.

Some Things to Take Away from Chapter 4

A Key Insight from Economics: There will be times when it makes sense to waste time, money, or effort to signal that you have some valuable or useful quality. But do not invest in a signal unless you are sure that the people who do not have that quality cannot or will not go through the trouble of sending the same signal.

A Valuable or Important Empirical Finding by Economists Who Study Signals: High school dropouts who invest in GED degrees are rewarded for the trouble they go through to get those degrees, even though there is no evidence to suggest they gain any valuable skill in the process of doing so.

When It Comes to Signaling, Dating Is a Lot Like:
Applying to college, trying to distinguish yourself in
the job market, pricing a company's stock at the IPO,
wishing someone "Happy Birthday."

Dating Advice: If you want to prove you are rich, burn a
big pile of money on the first date.

5

STATISTICAL DISCRIMINATION

Stereotypes

Though my ex-wife and I did not rush to finalize our divorce, we had no plans to reconcile. By the time I joined Match.com, I was divorced in every way except the legal one. So, when I posted a profile on Match.com, I listed myself as "Separated," and I wrote a simple, honest, and incredibly naive description of myself in which I explained that I was recently separated and looking for a new relationship.

What I didn't think about is that most men who are recently separated fall into one of the following three categories:

- Type 1: Enthusiastic returnees to the world of dating looking to have fun with, and be incredibly nice to, interesting women they've never met before.

- Type 2: Men who might go back to their wives (or, worse yet, haven't even left them).

- Type 3: Devastated wrecks who are angry and bitter about their failed marriage.

I wanted to be a Type 1, and let's assume for the moment I was. There was absolutely no way for women poring over Match.com profiles to distinguish me from the many men out there who were Type 2 or Type 3. And women looking for dates on Match.com believe the probability of a separated man being Type 2 or 3 is quite high.

The response to my initial profile was not overwhelming— even by middle-aged, balding economist standards. The vast majority of the e-mails I sent to women were ignored. One woman wrote back and said that, while she appreciated my honesty, she did not date recently separated men because she had found that they were not ready for a new relationship. Another woman wrote back and said that she was conflicted because, while my profile tended to indicate that I was exactly the type of person she would typically want to meet, she would not date separated men. She consoled me by noting that she also did not date men who had never been married because she thought that showed them to be incapable of maintaining a long-term relationship. (I guess you could call them Type 4s.)

In what was, by my standards, a remarkably flirtatious and successful string of follow-up e-mails, I convinced this woman to meet me for coffee so that I could show her that her preconceptions of separated men did not apply. But on the morning of the arranged date, she sent me a text that read, "Ultimately, I just am not comfortable dating a separated man. Thanks for your honesty. Good luck." By the way, compliments for honesty are a very small consolation in online dating.

While most people would say these women acted on a stereotype based on my separated status, the economics terminology would say I was a victim of *statistical discrimination*. Women who will not date separated men are not discriminating against separated men in the sense that they like them less or think separated men are bad. After all, these same women will date divorced men, all of whom were separated at some point. But they discriminate against separated men because of the *association* between being separated and being a Type 2 or Type 3.

This is a much less nefarious use of the term *discrimination* than you are used to. This feature of statistical discrimination—the fact that people act in a manner that hurts members of a certain group though they have no negative feelings toward that group—is what distinguishes it from *taste-based discrimination*. Jim Crow laws in the old South, for example, were a form of taste-based discrimination. The white people who made and enforced these rules did not want to associate with black people simply because they were black.

What made women's reaction to my online status statistical discrimination is that the women used "Separated" as a way to screen people who were likely to have qualities they dislike. I wasn't a victim of discrimination—I was a victim of a lack of information.

I tried to address this lack of information in a few ways. I could not lie and claim to be divorced (i.e., cheap talk—see chapter 2). Instead, I provided *more* information by adding a disclaimer to my Match.com profile in which I explained that, while I was still technically married, this was a legal formality and I was emotionally the equivalent of divorced. Second, I provided *less* information by branching out and using a second dating website: OkCupid. OkCupid profiles do not include marital status. The women who saw my profile there were unaware of my marital status until they either asked me directly (which nobody ever did) or I disclosed it. I generally explained my marital status one of the first few times I met a woman, waiting until I was sure the person knew I was not a Type 2 or Type 3, but not waiting so long that it would seem like I had been trying to hide something.

I have a friend who returned to the dating scene a few years ahead of me after a somewhat longer hiatus. As a widower after a thirty-plus year marriage, he benefited from statistical discrimination that worked in his favor. This friend is an extremely interesting and fun person. But he's had a few health issues, and he's a bit … well, let's just say his Match.com profile cannot credibly claim that he is "Athletic and Toned." Nonetheless, his profile made him seem like a very, very likely Type 1. His e-mails to women on Match.com were generally returned, and he received many unsolicited e-mails and winks because the assumptions women made about him were positive.

Statistical Discrimination Is Everywhere and Affects Almost Everyone

The statistical discrimination against my separated status led to some mild inconvenience for me and limited the pool of women I could choose from. But statistical discrimination can be much more damaging in other contexts. Let's consider common examples of statistical discrimination that impose real costs on the equivalents of the Type 1s who cannot easily distinguish themselves from the Type 2 and Type 3 people who, due to lack of specific information, they are pooled with.

- Example 1: When people drive through low-income neighborhoods, they often lock their car doors despite having driven long distances in other areas with the doors unlocked. This is because they see poor people and, though they are not prejudiced against poor people per se, they associate people who are poor with those who are more likely to commit crime.

- Example 2: When hiring for a job where many of the candidates are in their twenties or thirties, firms will often prefer male candidates to female candidates, because women of that age are more likely to leave their jobs or take extended leaves of absence to have children. This is a perfectly rational belief on the part of the employers, given that the average time a woman of that age holds a job is less than a similar man's. However, it is extremely frustrating for all women, especially those that have no plans to bear children. Women who do not plan to have children are pooled with women who do plan to have children and, as a result, deemed less desirable by employers.

- Example 3: Men are sometimes discriminated against in hiring because, as a group, they are much more likely to commit crimes than women are. Also, given that young, uneducated men are much less attached to the work force than they used to be, employers sometimes make assumptions about the work ethic of lower-skilled men. I recently interviewed a small business owner in the Midwest (not the one who explained signaling so well in chapter 4) who needed to hire people to work in a warehouse. The work did not require a great deal of skill, but it did require working hard and not stealing the valuable merchandise in the company's inventory. When I asked why the warehouse work was never done on a night shift, the owner told me, "Your best workers on the line here are single moms with a couple of kids and a deadbeat husband. And if you run a night shift, then they won't work for you and you got their deadbeat husbands here working. And so if we can keep those hours to work for them, we got better workers." There are surely plenty of low-skilled men who would be great at these jobs, but this business owner statistically discriminates against them. Again, he doesn't care that they are men—he cares that men are, in his experience, *more likely* to be crooked employees.

- Example 4: Twenty-year-old men typically pay higher car insurance premiums than twenty-year-old women with equivalent driving records and otherwise similar characteristics. There are many twenty-year-old men who drive extremely cautiously, but insurance companies do not watch them driving and so, lacking information on their specific driving habits, cannot judge them by their own record. Because, *on average*, twenty-year-old men drive faster and more erratically than twenty-year-old women, these men are statistically discriminated against, even though the insurance company has no animus towards men.

- Example 5: "Racial profiling" is essentially statistical discrimination. The highway patrol is accused of pulling over more minority drivers, and Arab airline passengers often get extra attention when going through airport security. Some of this scrutiny is likely the result of taste-based discrimination, in that the police may be hostile to minorities and use their power to harass drivers from these groups. But it could also be the case that police officers are not hostile to minorities and airport security workers are not hostile to Arabs, yet they believe (with at least some empirical justification) that race is positively correlated with the things they have been empowered to control (crime in the case of the police, and terrorism on airplanes in the case of airport security).

All of these are examples of rational statistical discrimination, or "true" stereotypes. Individuals in each of these groups will be different, but the assumptions people make about each group are based on actual statistical relationships. As these examples make clear, statistical discrimination is going on all around us every day. But, while the word *discrimination* conjures up images of unfairness and blameworthy behavior, a lot of statistical discrimination is tolerated. Why does the world think it is okay for women to snub separated men while there is outrage about racial profiling at airports and on highways? Why do customers tolerate gender-based insurance rates while statistically discriminating against women in hiring is a violation of civil rights law?

There are two answers to explain this distinction, I think. The first isn't very economics-oriented. Simply, there are some forms of statistical discrimination that seem fair and some that don't. Few people can conjure up a great deal of sympathy for separated men who have a somewhat smaller selection of potential dates and who, after waiting a little while, will move into the "Divorced" category. But when statistical discrimination is against a group (women, minorities, Arabs) whose members have no control over their status, it strikes most people as unfair. One could argue that men should qualify for sympathy on their car insurance rates, since they do not choose their gender. But, either because people believe men have enough advantages in life to compensate for the car insurance expense or because men grow out of the extra insurance cost as they age, gender-based insurance pricing has generated relatively little opposition.

The second distinction between acceptable and unacceptable statistical discrimination relates to economic *efficiency*—that is, the degree to which statistical discrimination makes society as a whole worse off rather than only making some people worse off to the benefit of some others. What would happen if the government mandated that gender could no longer be used as a factor in determining car insurance rates? The incentives to drive safely to keep rates low would be the same. Young men would save some money and young women would lose some money. A few men who could not afford to buy insurance before would now be able to afford it, and a few women would now be priced out of the market. Young men would benefit, roughly offset by the costs to young women, with little or no effect on insurance company profits. We would have approximately the same number of drivers, the same accident rate, and the same level of profit for insurers.

But now think about a firm choosing among several job candidates in their twenties, where some candidates are men and some are women. What happens if the firm chooses a man for the job because the hiring manager thinks that the man is more likely to stay on the job for a longer time than a similar woman? The direct effects on the parties involved are essentially zero sum—the man who gets the job is a little better off, and the woman that would otherwise have gotten it is a little worse off.

If that were the only effect, we might think it was unfair, but we would not think it was inefficient—the good and the bad effects would balance out. But now transport the woman who did not get this job back in time a few years to her college days. If she understood that her career prospects would be limited because employers could make gender-based assumptions about her qualifications for a job, she might work less hard or stay in school for fewer years. That is, anticipating a low return on her investment in college, she would reduce that investment. This decision might keep her from making an investment in her education that would have paid off if she were able to credibly convince potential employers that she would remain active in the labor force. The woman is hurt, but so is the economy in general—she did not make an investment that would have paid off for her and for society as a whole.

Laws and Courts Fight *Some* Statistical Discrimination

Because it is an obstacle of fairness and efficiency, statistical discrimination is illegal in several contexts. In justifying guidelines developed by the Civil Rights Division of the Justice Department to stop racial profiling, Attorney General John Ashcroft cited fairness (calling it "wrong") and efficiency (saying it "undermines law enforcement by undermining the confidence that people can have in law enforcement").

Statistical discrimination in the job market is illegal under the Civil Rights Act of 1964 (Title VII), which states that employers may not discriminate against an employee or potential employee when hiring, firing, promoting, and so on. The Equal Employment Opportunity Commission (EEOC) makes it clear that this policy includes statistical discrimination, rather than just taste-based discrimination, defining discriminatory practices to include "employment decisions based on stereotypes or assumptions about the abilities, traits, or performance of individuals of a certain sex, race, age, religion, or ethnic group." Note that the rule does not distinguish between valid and invalid assumptions and stereotypes, so employers may not statistically discriminate, even if they do so based on beliefs about differences in groups that are supported by demographics.

Companies can sometimes get around these rules (and, as a result, statistically discriminate). One way to exclude some potential employees is to set qualifications for jobs that may exclude members of one group in greater proportion than other groups. For example, firms are free to exclude applicants with criminal records despite the fact that doing so excludes far more men than women; they can require the ability to lift a certain amount of weight despite the fact that this excludes more women than men; and they can require a college degree even though doing so excludes a substantially larger portion of African American and Native American candidates than whites or Asian Americans. There is sometimes a fine line, however, between when a job qualification is necessary and when it crosses the line to be statistical discrimination, which has led to important legal cases regarding this phenomenon of *disparate impact*.

In the 1971 landmark case *Griggs v. Duke Power Company*, the Supreme Court ruled that companies cannot hire in a way that has a disparate impact on a specific group of workers. Duke Power had a plant in Draper, North Carolina, which, prior to the passage of the Civil Rights Act in 1964, explicitly limited certain jobs to white workers with a high school diploma. In 1965, it stopped prohibiting African Americans from holding those jobs, thereby ending its policy of discrimination. But the plaintiffs in the case held that African Americans were still discriminated against because the high school diploma requirement remained in place. They argued that many people without high school diplomas were qualified for the position and that African American candidates were much less likely to hold high school diplomas. That is, they claimed that the statistical discrimination should not be allowed because it was based on a false assumption (or an incorrect stereotype—that candidates without high school diplomas were less qualified for this job.) The court agreed with this claim, specifically focusing on the lack of evidence clearly connecting holding a high school diploma to better job performance. The decision put the onus on employers to show a "business necessity" for job requirements.

If "Separated" men were a protected class in online dating analogous to groups protected under employment discrimination law, it would be illegal for women to consider marital status when choosing whom to date. So women might set up another means of distinguishing the Type 2 and Type 3 men from the Type 1s. For example, a woman might say she would not date any man who had not had a serious relationship since he and his wife split up. But if *Griggs'* disparate impact logic applied to online dating, women could apply that filter only if they could show that having had a relationship after marriage is a truly important factor in determining who is a Type 1 man. Luckily for *almost* all involved, the Supreme Court does not get involved in such matters, and separated men are left to fend for themselves.

Statistical Discrimination Affects Wages

If my experience is representative, separated men get fewer replies to online date requests than divorced or widowed men. This may be analogous to the fact that women still make less money than men do, on average, even after adjusting for differences in education, work experience, and the like. It's very hard to prove to what degree the male-female wage gap can be attributed to statistical discrimination, but statistical discrimination could well be an important contributing factor. As I already noted, the fact that a woman's average expected duration in a job is shorter than an otherwise equivalent man's induces some firms to prefer to hire men. But the firm could also work this out through wages. If allowed, the firm will offer a lower wage to a woman than it would to a man with the same background.

The male-female wage difference will be greater when a firm thinks a female employee is more likely to leave the job (which the firm might estimate based on attempts to determine whether she plans to have children, whether her husband holds a job that would require him to move, etc.). But, unless the firm has excellent information of this kind, it will always offer the woman at least a somewhat lower wage.

While I already noted that this discrimination affects women before they even enter the workforce, the effects can be quite large because they feed on themselves. Women who think there will be a good chance that they will leave their jobs after a short time to have children will be less inclined to work hard while they are in school. This leads to a situation in which women, because of the choices they make based on what they expect firms to do, *are* less qualified (on average). The situation is thus worse for all women because, even conditional on their education, women will be less well trained and less productive than men. Therefore, women— including those who have every intention of staying at the firm for a long time—are discriminated against for two reasons. First, they have the direct problem of not being able to show that they intend to stay on the job a long time. Second, they have the indirect problem of being *assumed* to have prepared less intensively for the job because other women, rationally responding to their own incentives, prepared less intensively.

Creative pay systems can solve this problem in some cases. Consider a situation in which men and women are, on average, expected to keep their jobs for an equally long time. But the firm may be better able to predict the intentions of potential male employees than female employees. To be more concrete, let's say all men stay on the job for exactly ten years and that half of the women quit after two years to have children and the other half stay on the job for eighteen years. Employers cannot tell which women will be the ones who leave quickly until they actually quit. In this case, the firm could simply make pay heavily dependent on seniority so that women who quit quickly earn relatively little, women who stay earn much more late in their careers, and the men make a predictable amount. The firm could base a pay system on seniority in which men and women made the same amount and the firm was equally happy to employ workers of either gender. Even in this system, though, a woman who is not sure about her pregnancy plans at the time she must decide what degree of education she wants to pursue would likely underinvest in herself and contribute to her own gender-based career limitations later on.

If employers do apply stereotypes when they hire workers, they should eventually judge employees once they get to know the specifics of the person (at least if the firm is open-minded). That is, firms "learn" about their employees. An interesting study by economists Joseph Altonji and Charles Pierret shows that firms make assumptions (i.e., statistically discriminate) based on education when they hire workers. Later on, however, when some employees turn out to be better than their backgrounds suggest while others turn out to be worse, companies adjust workers' career trajectories to their individual abilities. The data shows that, over time, employees' wages become more dispersed as their background characteristics become a weaker indicator of their productivity than their on-the-job performance. Altonji and Pierret find strong evidence that firms statistically discriminate based on education by showing that, over time, education becomes a much weaker predictor of wages, while other measures of ability that are not initially known to employers (for example, IQ test results) become much more closely related to wages.

These results are actually glad tidings, in that statistical discrimination wears off slowly in the labor market for those who hang in there and get a chance to show their true ability. The downside of statistical discrimination goes away in the online dating market, too, but for a very different reason—separated people generally become divorced at some point.

Statistical Discrimination Affects Prices

There have been a number of very interesting recent studies of discrimination in product markets. For example, Ian Ayres and Peter Siegelman sent people of different races and genders to car dealers to negotiate new car purchases. They found that white men were offered lower prices than white women, and *much* lower prices than African Americans. There is no way to tell, however, whether this was due to taste-based or statistical discrimination on the part of the car dealers. The lower prices offered to white men could have been because the dealers found interacting with African American people unpleasant and would only transact business with them if compensated through higher prices (which would be taste-based discrimination). Alternatively, they may have assumed that African American buyers were less adept negotiators and tried to milk them for a higher price (which would be statistical discrimination, possibly based on faulty assumptions).

Three recent studies have used clever mechanisms to separate taste-based and statistical discrimination in common product market interactions. John List started with an exercise very similar to what Ayres and Siegelman did with car dealers, only he sent people of different races, genders, and ages to buy a Ken Griffey baseball card at sports memorabilia shows. He did the same thing on the sell side of the market, looking at the prices for this baseball card received by members of the different groups. List's results were very similar to those of Ayres and Siegelman—white males received the most favorable treatment from the people they dealt with. They received the best initial offers and, after some negotiation, the best final prices. Knowing that the sports-card dealers exhibited some form of discrimination in their actions, List then recruited many of these dealers to participate in various laboratory experiments where he could determine if the dealers exhibited taste-based discrimination. List performed multiple experiments in which the dealers were given numerous opportunities to exhibit taste-based discrimination in such a way that nobody (including List himself) would know which dealer showed prejudice. But he found no evidence of animus toward minorities, suggesting that the behavior he saw at the card-trading shows was statistical discrimination driven by the expectation that minorities would be willing to pay more for cards they wanted or accept less for cards they were trying to sell.

One limit of List's study is that participants in card markets are a small and not necessarily representative part of the economy. Two other recent studies have tried to look at somewhat broader markets. Asaf Zussman studied the discrimination of Jewish Israelis (who make up a majority in the country) against the Arab minority. He sent a pair of messages to each of eight thousand Jewish people who had listed cars for sale on Israel's largest classified ads website (the Israeli equivalent of Craigslist.) Each pair of messages was basically identical, except that one was signed "Moshe" (a distinctly Jewish name) and one was signed "Muhammad" (a distinctly Arab one). The e-mails offered a price for the car that was a discount relative to the price listed in the advertisement. Zussman found substantial evidence of discrimination, as the response rate to Jewish buyer e-mails was much higher than the response rate to Arab buyers; an Arab buyer who offered to pay the price listed in the advertisement and a Jewish buyer who offered a 5 to 10 percent discount were equally likely to hear back from the seller.

Zussman then called each of the car sellers and administered an apparently unrelated survey that asked numerous questions about their feelings about Arabs and Arab/Jewish relations. The car sellers had no idea (or, at least they were not informed) that there was a connection between their car sale and the phone survey. Zussman then matched the individuals' survey responses to their responses to e-mails from prospective buyers. The respondents in the survey revealed negative views of Arabs along several dimensions, with many indicating that they thought Arabs were of lower natural intelligence than Jews and should be forced to use segregated recreational facilities. However, the degree to which individuals showed discrimination against Arabs in the car negotiations was correlated with only one question on the survey—the degree to which they agreed with the statement, "The Arabs in Israel are more likely to cheat than the Jews." So, while Jews express negative feelings about Arabs in Israel, they are able to put these feelings aside when transacting sales with Arabs as long as they do not expect to get cheated. That is, Zussman's study indicates that Jews discriminate against Arabs when transacting business because they think more Arabs are cheaters, *not* because they do not like Arabs.

The final study, which was carried out in the United States by Jennifer Doleac and Luke Stein, also involved listings on an online classified site (either Craigslist or something similar). Doleac and Stein posted numerous ads selling new iPods on three hundred different geographical subdivisions of the website. The advertisements were similar in terms of the product offered, the suggested price, and the other written portions of the listings. The ads varied, however, in their visual presentation—some showed the iPods being held by a dark-skinned hand and forearm, some showed them being held by a white hand and tattooed forearm, and others showed them held by a white hand and clear forearm. The ads featuring the darker arm garnered fewer offers and lower prices being offered. Though this result could have been due (at least partly) to taste-based discrimination, several features of the replies to these ads suggested the differences were largely due to statistical discrimination. First, these ads received roughly the same responses as the ads featuring the tattooed arm. Doleac and Stein hypothesize that negative views against tattoos are unlikely to be due to taste-based discrimination, suggesting that the similar responses to tattoos and African Americans are driven by statistical discrimination. Second, they find the effects largest in areas where people are less exposed to African American people or where minority crime rates are highest, suggesting buyers are simply afraid of African Americans, rather than hostile to them.

Naturally, this is a very sobering example. I'm sorry I was statistically discriminated against on dating sites, but being a middle-aged white male makes me otherwise very lucky in terms of the assumptions that are made about me. I pay the price for being "Separated," but I reap the benefits on my car insurance and will get a good price if I ever want to sell my iPod or my car.

Some Things to Take Away from Chapter 5

A Key Insight from Economics: People of a given color, gender, age, or marital status will be discriminated against in many situations, even when the people doing the discriminating hold no animus toward members of that group.

Hostility or ill feeling

A Valuable or Important Empirical Finding by Economists Who Study Statistical Discrimination: When buying or selling cars, iPods, and other items, people make assumptions about the buyer or seller that have exactly the same economic effects as if they had hateful feelings driven by racism, sexism, and the like.

When It Comes to Statistical Discrimination, Dating Is a
Lot Like: Buying car insurance, deciding whether or not
to go shopping in a dangerous area, worrying about being
racially profiled.

Dating Advice: Finalize your divorce quickly.

6

THICK VERSUS THIN MARKETS

Big Fish or Big Pond?

As an experiment, I logged into Match.com and got a list of the women between forty and fifty who live within ten miles of me. I was presented with 454 women. I did the same thing on Date.com, and I was given 134 women to choose from. Does it matter which site I use? It seems like both have plenty of options for me.

Now consider a third option. I play a lot of tennis. It would be nice to meet a woman who shared this interest, so I logged into TennisDate.com and searched for all women between forty and fifty years old who live in California. I was presented with 52 options, nine of whom were within a one-hour drive of my house. That's a much smaller set to choose from, but at least they all share an interest of mine. I also pretended to be a vegetarian (I am not, but I'm willing to imagine for a few minutes—I would draw the line at pretending to be vegan). There were twenty-two women between forty and fifty living within twenty miles of me on VeggieDate.com.[1]

Finally, what if I try to meet women in person instead of over the internet? Living in an area with a lot of well-educated people, I'm lucky to live near a couple of high-quality bookstores. Each of these hosts a book club where patrons can meet to discuss a work of fiction. Now, I'll admit that I have never been to one of these clubs, so I can't make any statements about their demographic composition with absolute certainty. But at the risk of being accused of statistical discrimination myself, I would bet that the vast majority of people who attend the meetings are female. I'd bet, too, that if I went to one of these meetings, I'd be the only man there and would meet about five women who are my age and single.

Which option is best—Match.com, Date.com, TennisDate.com, or the book club? In this case, size matters. Having more women available obviously increases the chances that I will find a good match. When you first think about the numbers, there doesn't seem to be a huge difference between 454 and 134. I couldn't possibly date 134 women in a reasonable period of time, much less 454. I narrowed down the 134 Date.com options to only 48, however, just by getting rid of drinkers, smokers, anyone with less than a college education,

---

1. You may think I am making this stuff up, but I'm not. Other specialized dating sites include FarmersOnly.com and Sugardaddie.com. Also, though I certainly do not condone using its services, marriedsecrets.com leads a surprisingly dense collection of sites that hook up married people. And, for those interested in a different kind of "thick" market, try largeandlovely.com.

and people with a few physical characteristics that I prefer to avoid. The first three said they wanted to have children, so they were eliminated. The next one was clearly lying about one of the physical characteristics I had attempted to screen for. The next one could not spell and began each part of her description with "Well . . . " Sorry, but even balding economists can afford to be a little picky.

Anyway, you get the idea. My original list of 134 women was, at best (that is, if I was willing to include the women whose favorite book was *Eat, Pray, Love*), going to lead to ten whom I would want to message. Based on my prior experience, I would guess that about three of the ten would write back, and maybe one of those three would eventually meet me for a first date. The fact that the "market" is three times larger on Match.com now looks much more important.

3/10
respond

While we can quickly see why the "supply" of women matters, the bookstore example shows why "demand" matters as well. Once I narrow down my search on Match.com or Date.com, I have to face the possibility that some other guys have already won over the women I am interested in. But at the book club, I'm a monopolist. I have only a few options, but I am the only game in town (at least for the length of the book discussion).

Thick Markets Make for Better Matches

The "size matters" issue is what economists refer to as a *thick market effect*. The more options there are in a market, the more likely a buyer or seller is to find a good match. Think about it this way. Suppose you were looking for a place to buy a pair of jeans. Where would you rather be if you had a single hour to shop—midtown Manhattan or the middle of a rural community? Of course you would rather be in Manhattan, because you would have access to numerous stores selling jeans. Not only could you find a pair of jeans in that hour, but you could probably find a pair that fit your taste and budget quite well. — *If you had Filters, then I agree.*

Thick markets in dating work the same way. On Match.com, I have three times as many options as I have on Date.com. Sure, I might find a woman who is a great match for me on the first try on Date.com. You never know. But the best match I can make on Match.com is likely to be better for me than the best match on Date.com.

Labor markets are another place where market size matters. Think about a software engineer looking for a job. Software engineering skills are in high demand just about everywhere; even in hard economic times, software engineers can generally find good job opportunities. The greater San Jose, California, metropolitan area (aka Silicon Valley) and the greater Kansas City, Missouri, area contain about the same number of people. But, all else being equal, a software engineer is likely to have a better job—in the sense that it fits her skills better and is more enjoyable for her—if she lives in Silicon Valley than if she lives in Kansas City. There are software companies and other employers of engineers in both areas, but in Silicon Valley there are a myriad of companies of all different sizes employing engineers to do every possible task you could ever think of asking an engineer to do. In Kansas City, the range of opportunities is substantial, but nowhere near that of Silicon Valley. For a software engineer who wants to do fairly general work and is not very picky about the size or type of company she works for, either place will be just as good. But if an engineer wants to be more specialized, either in the type of work she does or the type of company she works for, she is likely to find a better match in Silicon Valley. The opportunity to develop and use a unique set of skills and interests will be greater there. So there are lots of engineers in Kansas City with great jobs—but, on average, they like their jobs a little less than the engineers in Silicon Valley.

Economists Hoyt Bleakley and Jeffrey Lin pored through a lot of census data to back up this "thicker markets lead to happier workers" idea. They showed that workers in more condensed metropolitan areas are less likely to switch the industry or the occupation in which they work. That is, workers in such areas switch the type of job that they hold less frequently, presumably because they are happier in the work they are able to find in big (thick) markets. But this effect takes time to develop over a person's career. In thicker markets, young workers are actually more likely to switch the type of job they have. These workers are taking advantage of the wider set of opportunities in bigger markets to shop around for the right job. But once they find that job, they are more likely to keep it.

Thick Markets Lead to More Specialization

So size matters and, all else being equal, a bigger dating site is better. But all else is not equal in this context. If I will consider dating only tennis players or vegetarians, then a much smaller set of potential dates from TennisDate.com or VeggieDate. com may well be better than the Match.com options. So how do I decide whether to be a generalist (that is, use Match.com) or a specialist (on the tennis or vegetarian sites)?

Specialist dating sites may well be the way to go if you are truly passionate about a particular aspect of your potential mate, but the local market size matters a lot here, as well. Let's assume that 5 percent of the people in a given area are vegetarians (a figure around the typical level for most Western countries). Then vegetarians rule out nineteen out of every twenty potential mates if they insist on partners who are also vegetarian. For a vegetarian who lives in Manhattan, this restriction limits his options considerably but should not be insurmountable, given that he lives within a few square miles of literally millions of other people. In that area, there have to be plenty of single female vegetarians. But a vegetarian in a small city is likely to find that he either has to compromise his insistence on dating only other vegetarians or compromise on some other dimension to find a partner. The bottom line, then, is that TennisDate.com and VeggieDate. com are much more viable options in densely populated areas where there are more people with this specialized interest packed into the region.

The concentration of gay people in urban areas is probably caused by a confluence of factors, but market thickness is surely a big one. Estimates vary, but fewer than 5 percent of people are self-declared to be exclusively homosexual. Living in a small town, then, is more limiting when searching for a same-sex partner than when looking for a mate of the opposite sex. While approximately 75 percent of American heterosexual couples live in an urban area, 85 percent of lesbian couples and 90 percent of gay male couples are in cities. The search for thicker markets is also likely to be at least part of why only a third of partners in same-sex couples were born in the same state, while for heterosexual couples the figure exceeds 50 percent.

Just as it behooves the online dater in a less populated area to be more of a "generalist," providers of services in less-populated areas also tend to be less specialized. Consider a doctor setting up a practice in Emporia, Kansas (population 24,916) versus a doctor in Palo Alto, California (which is part of a metropolitan area with millions of people). There are plenty of doctors in Emporia, but there are no dermatologists and just two orthopedic surgeons. People in Emporia who want such specialized services must drive more than an hour to Topeka or Wichita.

The market in Emporia is simply not big enough for a dermatologist to set up shop, and as a result, the residents do not have a thick market of dermatologists or orthopedic surgeons from which to choose. On the other hand, there are eighteen dermatologists and ten orthopedic surgeons at my local medical clinic in Palo Alto (and many more at other nearby facilities). My son and I alone have been referred to specialists within each of these groups depending on the nature of our current broken bone or skin condition, respectively. People in Emporia break bones and are just as susceptible to sun damage as we are in Palo Alto. But, because they are in a smaller market, they have to rely more on the care of doctors with less specialized training or drive to a thicker market for their medical care.

The same principle applies to specialists in other markets. Economists Luis Garicano and Thomas Hubbard studied the market for legal services, using data from all across the United States, and found that lawyers and law firms are more specialized in larger markets. So the typical lawyer in Emporia is likely to do a broader range of legal work than the typical lawyer in Topeka, even though the two cities are only an hour apart. Or, thought of another way, you are likely to call the same lawyer in Emporia if you get arrested, want to sell your house, or are getting divorced. But, in Topeka, you would call a different lawyer for each situation.

Yukako Ono showed that market thickness more broadly led to specialization of all business services, in that firms in thicker local markets are likely to outsource activities such as advertising and bookkeeping. In bigger markets, firms that specialize in these areas can survive. But in smaller markets, they cannot, so firms have to do such tasks themselves.

Thick Markets Don't Necessarily Have More Intense Competition

Now we return to the issue of whether I should even bother with online dating at all, or rather just trawl for women where the men don't go. Local book clubs have the potential to provide a supply of intelligent women with virtually no competition. And even if I don't find the woman of my dreams, I can at least get a good book discussion out of it. (I'm willing to admit it—I read and enjoyed *The Help*. I did, however, ask the woman I was dating at the time to act like she dragged me there when we went to see the movie.)

In the end, there shouldn't be much of a difference between the two platforms for meeting women, at least in terms of the probability of finding a match over time. Competition (that is, other men) will move between the different venues (both physical and virtual) where eligible women hang out until the success rate is roughly equal across the various options.

Rather than thinking about where to get a date, think about where to get customers if you are setting up a store. Naturally you would like to be where the customers are. So, by the same logic that shoppers would rather look for jeans in Manhattan than in a rural town, you would probably think that a store would rather set up shop in Manhattan than in that same rural town. If it were the first store, that would surely be correct. But if stores are free to open when they think doing so is profitable and close when they are losing money, then stores will open, close, and move such that they are equally profitable just about anywhere.

Suppose, for example, that you were trying to decide where to open a new lighting store back in the 1980s. At the time, there was an area in the Bowery part of Lower Manhattan known as the Lighting District. I remember being amazed as I walked through this area that store after store sold nothing but lights. People who needed lights knew that there was a very thick market there and would pay the district a visit. So someone who wanted to open a light store would face the question of whether to open in this very competitive but large market or, for example, to open on the Upper West Side and be the only lighting store within a several-block radius. Or to use the metaphor from this chapter's subtitle, the potential store owner had to decide whether to be a big fish in a small pond or a small fish in a big pond. Over time, lighting stores opened and shut, so that while there remained a large cluster of stores in that one area, lighting stores were about equally profitable wherever they were in Manhattan.

The thickness of the Lighting District market has been thinned out considerably, however, because another thick market for lighting has risen to take its place. While the most convenient way to see lots of lighting options in a short time used to be to amble through the Lighting District, you can now do essentially the same thing in your own home on the internet. As a result of that development and other forces, the number of lighting stores in the area has been cut approximately in half over the last fifteen years.

Though I know of no hard data to back this up, the story of the Lighting District suggests that the rise of internet dating has been tough on singles bars. As the thickest market for singles has become the internet, some bars may well be feeling the pressure.

Where Should You Open Your Store?

While I like to use internet dating as an example of all things economic, that market was not available to Stanford mathematician Harold Hotelling in 1929. Hotelling, invading the turf of economists, wrote a classic paper about competition that explored where stores should open in a hypothetical scenario.

Hotelling wrote about a boardwalk that runs along a straight line from point A to point B. Suppose we have one person who sells ice cream from a cart, and he wants to set up shop somewhere along the boardwalk. Let's assume that people are spread out roughly evenly along the boardwalk and that everyone with an urge for ice cream goes to the ice cream cart nearest to him. When there is only one cart, it doesn't really matter where the vendor sets up. All customers on the boardwalk come to his cart.

But what happens when there are two carts? You might think that they would each set up near the ends of the boardwalk and split the market. But if they did that, each would have an incentive to move his cart a little closer to the middle. By doing so, he'd capture a bit more of the market near the middle of the boardwalk while not giving up any of the market near the end where he originally set up. In fact, the only way both vendors have an incentive to keep their carts stable (or, in economic-speak, the only *equilibrium*) is for both carts to be set up side by side in the dead center of the boardwalk. That's fine for the vendors, since they split the market. But it is not good for customers, who could save travel time if the vendors separated a bit.

If a third vendor shows up with another ice cream cart, all hell breaks loose. When there are three or more vendors, they can literally never find a way to set up so that they are all happy. At least one of them will be constantly moving her cart to try to get more customers. While the image of ice cream vendors endlessly running around a boardwalk seems comical, it's not a terrible metaphor for people pursuing each other in the online and physical dating markets. As more women go to book clubs, men begin to feign interest in the club. But then, as too many men get into the club, others drop out and try their luck at the singles bar instead. And so it goes, as each seeker looks for the thickest market and, in the process, also affects the thickness of that market.

Some Companies Locate Where
the Things They Buy Are

Luckily, most businesses are not as easy to move as ice cream carts, or customers would waste a lot of time running around looking for vendors. Most companies stay put and hope they have chosen the right place for customers to find them. But they don't necessarily pick a site near the customer. In fact, lots of companies pick their location based on the markets for the things they buy rather than for the things they sell.

Why? Let's think about three different businesses you might go into—carbon black, wine making, and carpet manufacturing. Carbon black is a very important material used in ways that I don't really understand to color and reinforce rubber and plastic. There is a lot of it in a tire, for example, and in your laser printer's toner. You use things that have carbon black in them all the time, though you probably never knew it. So where will a carbon black business set up? You might think it would want to be near a tire manufacturer or other big users of carbon black. But because the main input to carbon black is natural gas, and most natural gas gets burned off in the production process, it makes sense to make carbon black near a natural gas source and then ship it to customers when it's finished. As a result, carbon black is largely manufactured in Texas, assuring that carbon black manufacturers have access to a thick market for their primary input and minimizing their transportation costs.

Wine, on the other hand, can be produced pretty much anywhere. You just need to buy grapevine cuttings, grow grapes, and set up a distillery. Wine is produced in all fifty states, in fact. There are even several wineries between my undergraduate college's remote campus in Vermont and the nearest airport, as I discovered with some friends after our most recent reunion. But while you can produce wine anywhere, experts (not me—I don't know a $10 bottle of wine from a Chateau Mouton Rothschild) agree that the best wine is produced from grapes grown in temperate, dry climates. So you can get wine in Vermont but, no disrespect intended to the places I stopped to do some tasting, not the best wine. California is a more natural place to grow wine and, as a result, about 90 percent of American wine is produced there. In this case, market thickness has little to do with where firms operate.

While we would say that there are natural reasons to set up your carbon black business or your wine business in a certain place, what about your carpet manufacturing operation? It turns out that if you were like just about every other carpet manufacturer, you would set up in (or near) Dalton, Georgia—"the Carpet Capital of the World." Finished carpet can be transported fairly cheaply, and because there is an extensive distribution channel in carpeting, the manufacturers need not be near the buyers (who, obviously, are spread out wherever people live). But—at least in the earlier days of carpet making—manufacturers needed yarn spinners and finishers, who were typically independent. And about the only place you can find these suppliers is in Dalton.

The reason for Dalton's carpet kingdom is not anything like the natural reasons to make carbon black in Texas or wine in California. It's really just a historical accident. Around 1900, a woman named Catherine Evans Whitener made a tufted bedspread—basically a fluffy blanket—that was unprecedented at the time. She started selling them and became very successful. Well, as luck would have it, the way Whitener made her bedspreads was, by 1950, more or less the best way to make modern carpets. As demand for carpet built quickly, the bedspread manufacturers of Dalton were well positioned to take advantage. They had a big pool of labor that could be easily redirected from making fluffy blankets to fluffy rugs. They also had a large group of spinners and finishers who could make the same transition. That is, carpet manufacturers set up plants in Dalton because the market for the goods they needed was thick there.

The historical accident that led to such a dense concentration of carpet makers in Dalton is not a unique example. While there are many natural reasons for firms of a certain type to cluster in a specific area, as in the carbon black and wine examples, there are also many cases where an early producer leads to an industry setting up in a certain area simply because it creates a thick market for labor and inputs. Detroit was the hub of the automobile industry for many years because Henry Ford set up his business there. But, like the carpet makers who started up in Dalton to take advantage of suppliers to the bedspread business, Ford set up in Detroit partly because so many suppliers to the carriage business were already located there. Similarly, Silicon Valley has become the hub of technology largely because Stanford's tradition in engineering has ensured a thick market for a key input of high-tech companies—technical staff.

Making a Market Thicker May Require Collective Action

Hopefully, by now you're convinced that thick markets lead to good matches and make shopping easy. However, just as all daters want a thick market of potential mates (Match.com) and no competition (the book club meeting), companies want a market thick with sellers and buyers (carbon black manufacturers in natural gas territory or lighting stores in the Bowery). But they also want the parties they transact with to think they are the only game in town—that is, firms want to be monopolists with plenty of customers to sell to and plenty of suppliers to buy from.

The incentive for individuals and firms to go in search of markets where they will not face competition can often create whole markets that are simply too thin. Think about a hospital looking for a gastroenterologist to join its staff. It's hard to find a good gastroenterologist. Each year, about three hundred are hired at hospitals across the United States, most of whom are finishing up a fellowship and taking their first position as full-fledged physicians. Suppose there was a "store" where you could go and shop for the available gastroenterologists, allowing hospitals and gastroenterologists to come together and find the best matches. It would essentially be a dating site for gastroenterologists and hospitals.

But now think of a hospital (let's call it General Hospital, or GH for short) that is a good place to work but maybe not the absolute best and most sought after. And suppose GH could move one step up the chain—*if* it could find a few of the really good gastroenterologists before they were put on display at the store. For example, maybe the head of GH's gastroenterology department has a friend who tells her of Adam, a great young gastroenterologist about to finish a fellowship where the friend works. So the hospital would go to Adam and say, "We would like you to join our staff. If you agree to it now, you can be guaranteed a good job and save yourself the time of going to the store. But you have to tell us yes or no today and, if you say no, we won't buy you in the store." This sly technique is widely known as an *exploding offer* in many labor markets.

Adam will no doubt find the exploding offer tempting, knowing that he may do worse if he tries his luck at the store. So he takes the position and never gets to see the thick market of buyers at the store. It may well work out for him, but he may also have unknowingly forgone a better option.

There are two problems with this bypassing of the store. First, because all the "buyers" and "sellers" of gastroenterologists do not get to see their full set of options, they end up agreeing to matches that are less than optimal. Some very good gastroenterologists end up working at hospitals that cannot appropriately employ their skills.

Second, the market may well unravel. Suppose the head of gastroenterology at Lexington Hospital (LH) is also a friend of the person who introduced Adam to the people at GH. The head of LH says to himself, "We are going to need a gastroenterologist next year, and I'd better get going on that soon. If I wait until the store opens, none of the good doctors will be left. And since everyone else knows that, they'll start looking soon, so I'd better get started before them." Before you know it, Adam finds he is getting calls from potential employers pretty much at the beginning of his gastroenterology fellowship. But all the callers insist he commit to the job right away or they will hire someone else. This pressure not only forces the young gastroenterologists to act early and make commitments they are not ready to make, it also reinforces the bad match problem because hospitals make offers before there has been enough time in the fellowship to determine who the top doctors will be.

This kind of unraveling happens all the time. I did not pick gastroenterology at random—it's one of the many markets for which economist Al Roth has tried to design systems that create increased efficiency. Roth's efforts to match gastroenterologists to hospitals, law clerks to judges, and kidney donors to kidney recipients (and many other examples) won him the Nobel Prize in economics in 2012. His work on gastroenterologists, which was done with Muriel Niederle, showed that the market for these doctors worked much more effectively from 1986 to 1996, when all the hospitals banded together and created a gastroenterology clearinghouse. In effect, they set up a gastroenterologist store and forbade doctors and hospitals to transact anywhere else. During the ten-year period while the "store" was open, gastroenterologists were more mobile, the market was national, and the decisions were made later.

Unfortunately, the market broke down in 1996, when there were not enough new gastroenterologists to go around. Suddenly, hospitals couldn't resist breaking their promise to wait until the store opened. A healthy, thick market turned into a chaotic thin market, and all those involved suffered. Basically, it was as if there were suddenly not enough single women available in the dating market, so a bunch of men started proposing on the first date and saying, "If you agree right now, we'll get married. But if you don't say yes tonight, I will never go on another date with you again."

Other markets unravel in similar ways or are kept from doing so by institutions put in place to insure that better decisions are made. For example, when the labor market is very hot, many employers find it hard to hire the graduates they want from top law and MBA programs. Individual firms, given the chance, will extend exploding offers to new students as they show up for their first days at these schools. Most schools protect their students from this practice by setting the timetable for when firms are allowed to begin the recruiting process, giving most students more and better options in the long run. Firms that want to stay in the schools' good graces generally adhere to their wishes.

One market that has been resistant to all thickening attempts, and which continues to unravel, is the market for appellate law clerks, which Al Roth and various coauthors have studied extensively. Among their numerous creative solutions to the unraveling problem is a proposal to randomly void some offers to clerks, preventing judges from being upset about having their offer rejected because the clerk may not have done it. But, despite at least some of Roth and his colleagues' suggestions being implemented, the market has remained quite stubborn—clerks are hired at the beginning of their second year of law school, a full two years before they begin the clerkships.

A great anecdote about the problems (and absurdity) of the unraveling law clerk market is related by one respondent to a survey by Roth and his colleagues. The clerk said, "I received the offer via voice mail while I was in flight to my second interview. The judge actually left three messages. First, to make the offer. Second, to tell me that I should respond soon. Third, to rescind the offer. It was a thirty-five-minute flight." Another said, "One of [Judge X's] clerks even chastised me for 'overly stringent adherence to this timeline they have' and noted that other students from my school were willing to interview ahead of schedule. It was a real conflict for me. I felt like I had to choose between cheating and (potentially) not getting a clerkship." Apparently, it's true—lawyers cannot keep their word, nor can they cooperate to act in the public good.

But the more important point, at least for our purposes, is that most of these judges seem to understand that they may not do well in a thick market. So they act early. And then others have to act early to beat the ones that will act early, and so on until the market turns very thin and disorderly. Just to be safe, I'm showing up a few hours early for the next book club.

Some Things to Take Away from Chapter 6

A Key Insight from Economics: Big markets allow for more customization. Specialty products, doctors, and lawyers are more common and more specialized in bigger cities.

A Valuable or Important Empirical Finding by Economists Who Study Market Thickness: People who live in larger metropolitan areas have a greater variety of job options. As a result, they job hop more when they are young and they keep a job longer when they are older.

When It Comes to Market Thickness, Dating Is a Lot Like: Deciding where to shop, deciding what kind of doctor or lawyer to be, picking a lamp.

Dating Advice: If you want your life partner to be a vegetarian, move to New York City.

7

ADVERSE SELECTION

Stigma

Online dating was growing rapidly but was still relatively new when Jennifer Egan wrote a *New York Times Magazine* cover story in November of 2003. According to the article, the pace of spending on online personals and online dating sites had grown by a factor of six in the previous three years. But not everybody was ready for this way of meeting people. Egan wrote, "A fair number of people still feel a stigma about online dating, ranging from the waning belief that it's a dangerous refuge for the desperate and unsavory to the milder but still unappealing notion that it's a public bazaar for the sort of people that thrive on selling themselves." In fact, the idea that only losers use dating services goes back a long way—at least to the first known computer dating service in the early 1960s. The ads for this pioneering dating service attacked this issue directly, saying "Some people think computer dating services attract only losers," then went on to explain the many attractive attributes of one of its clients.

Why do paid matchmaking services carry this stigma? Think about potential daters as belonging to one of two groups—those who are desirable and those who are not. People who are desirable can generally find mates using standard methods, such as meeting people at work, meeting people at school, or being fixed up by friends. But undesirable people can't use those methods because the people they interact with on a daily basis have recognized their nondesirability and will not enter into a relationship with them, nor enthusiastically recommend them to their friends. If the undesirable people know that they are undesirable, then this fact is *hidden information* when they first meet someone else. Roger, our friend from chapter 2, knew he was undesirable and clearly had no reason to advertise it.

The stigma of online dating came from this hidden information problem. If desirable people could find a partner the old-fashioned way, there would be only undesirable people on dating sites. People revealed their type by dating online. Taken to its extreme, nobody who believed him- or herself to be somewhat desirable would ever choose to join an online dating site. The online dating market would essentially collapse, and desirable people would continue to meet one another the old-fashioned way.

Buyer Beware: Buying a Used Car or Picking a Date

Hidden information problems are certainly not limited to the world of dating. George Akerlof received a Nobel Prize in economics for his pioneering work on problems of hidden information, or *adverse selection* in economics terminology. The key insight of Akerlof's analysis was that hidden information can lead to markets where only the least desirable goods trade hands. Akerlof focused on used cars in his work. He started by thinking about two types of used cars: *lemons*, which have problems and will be in the shop regularly, and *plums*, which still run without issue.

Used-car buyers are willing to pay more for a plum than for a lemon, of course. Imagine a very stark world, though, in which the sellers of used cars know whether the car they are selling is a lemon or a plum but the buyers cannot tell them apart. Because sellers know the difference between the types is indistinguishable to buyers, there will be one price for all used cars. In this market, owners of plums will not be willing to part with perfectly good cars, since the fixed price will reflect that many of the cars on the market are likely to be lemons. The outcomes on the used car market become self-fulfilling—*all* cars on the market are lemons because the plum buyers will not sell for the going rate.

And that is the very essence of adverse selection—if sellers have hidden information, they will offer only the unattractive merchandise for sale. Sadly, the same forces that make the available used cars disproportionately likely to be lemons could also have made the people who used early dating services likely to be loners or losers. Or, thought of another way, just as there is a certain stigma to selling a used car that you cannot prove is a plum, there was a stigma to being unable to find a partner through standard methods of networking. In both cases, the "seller" of the good (whether that good was a car or the dater himself) revealed private information about the good's quality through the way he sold it.

I Am a Lemon

Fortunately, the stigma associated with online dating has largely disappeared over time. While it was initially perceived that only desperate people would use online dating, others began to realize that online dating sites provided a rich source of potential mates and many of the other advantages already discussed. A recent study by psychologists reached the conclusion that "online dating has entered the mainstream, and it is fast shedding any lingering social stigma." So I don't have to worry about adverse selection issues when I go online. Or do I?

While online dating sites may not have a stigma associated with them, I have another problem. I am single and I am in my late forties. What does that tell you? One interpretation is that I am the result of adverse selection because I couldn't sustain a marriage or couldn't even develop a long-term relationship in the first place. In this case, the private information is that I am incapable of a long-term relationship and, though I'd like to hide that fact, it is revealed by my presence on the dating market.

Two things mitigate this particular form of adverse selection. First, there may be perfectly good reasons that a man or woman my age has not had a lifetime relationship, though we are capable of it. Essentially, just as the stigma of online dating has eroded over time, so has the stigma of divorce and delayed marriage. People largely understand that choices made early in life may not be optimal and that we change over time. Second, to the extent that being older and available is an indication of something negative, it is a trait I share with the women I date.

Unfortunately, a much more problematic adverse selection dynamic occurs in the job market. In that case, an unemployed person may have trouble finding a job because potential employers read a lot into the fact that the person is unemployed. Many job listings explicitly state that people who have been out of work for a while should not apply (or at least that currently employed people are preferred). One recruiter told the *New York Times* that his clients are "looking for someone who's gainfully employed, who's closer to the action." A woman who had been out of work for six months said, "I feel like I am being shunned by our entire society"; one recruiter told the woman that her spell of unemployment made her a "hard sell," despite her impressive skills.

Numerous economic studies have shown that job applicants have more trouble finding a new job as their spell of unemployment gets longer. This finding can be explained by reasons other than stigma, but the previous example (and many others like it) suggests that employers believe people who have trouble finding a job have trouble for a reason. Unemployment, just like being single, becomes a self-reinforcing state—employers figure that the fact that the jobless person has been passed up by other employers implies something about his skills.

Economists Robert Gibbons and Lawrence Katz provide another interesting way to think about adverse selection in the labor market. They studied workers who had lost their jobs, grouping them into two categories—those whose employer had permanently shut the facility and those whose employer had downsized but continued operations. Their hypothesis was that there should be no stigma to losing a job because a company shuts down. These people were just in the wrong place at the wrong time and there is no reason to think that they were bad at their jobs, with the possible exception of those who ran the company.

Gibbons and Katz expected there to be a stigma for employees who were downsized, however, because their employers chose to get rid of them while keeping others. This decision revealed some hidden information to the market because, by choosing specific people to be downsized, the firms essentially said, "This is not one of my more important employees."

Sure enough, Gibbons and Katz found evidence of adverse selection—those who were downsized took longer to find jobs and were paid less once they did than those whose facility was closed. The labor market appears to interpret getting downsized as a negative piece of private information held by the previous employer, leaving downsized workers to carry this stigma until they can prove themselves elsewhere. Or, thought of another way, just as someone who had to use a dating service is assumed to have been dumped for a reason, workers who are laid off while the firm continues operating are assumed to have been let go for a reason.

Adverse Selection of Customers

Just as you want to be careful not to pick a lemon on Match.com and companies carefully try to avoid hiring lemons as employees, firms also have to be careful not to pick (or be picked by) customers who turn out to be lemons. How can someone who buys a company's products be a lemon? Some customers are more expensive to serve than others. Usually that's not a problem—the company can build the cost difference into its prices. But if a company cannot determine which customers are the more expensive ones, it has to offer a single price. This leads to adverse selection when the customers who are most expensive to serve are also the ones who value the product the most.

Product market adverse selection has been a big part of the health-care public policy debates that have been going on in the Unites States and elsewhere for the last few decades. Let's take a simple example, based loosely on a couple of people I know. Carleton and Douglas are forty-year-old men, they are both in good shape, and the results of their physical exams would look identical to an insurance company. However, Douglas is a hypochondriac and, unbeknownst to the insurance company, has a family history of heart disease. The insurance company knows that the average forty-year-old man with exams similar to Carleton's and Douglas's will cost the company about $10,000 in medical expenditures each year, so it wants to set its premium a bit higher than that so it makes some profit.

But now think about Carleton. He's the healthier one and he's not a hypochondriac, so he knows that he's likely to only spend about $5,000 on health care in a year. If he buys insurance, he gets some peace of mind in case something terrible happens. But he also wastes, on average, over $5,000. Meanwhile, Douglas knows that he will spend lots of time visiting his clinic and getting doctors to run lots of tests. So he expects expenditures of at least $15,000 in a typical year, making the $10,000 premium a bargain.

This leaves the insurance company in a tough spot—healthy people see no reason to buy insurance and the sick people are unprofitable. In other words, the company is the victim of adverse selection. The insurer has no choice but to raise its rates to at least $15,000, a price at which only the very sickest patients buy insurance. Private information, then, does not just lead to only undesirable people using online dating sites and only the worst used cars getting traded. It also leads to only the sickest people buying insurance.

Recent health-care policy debates in the United States and many other countries have focused on the need for an *individual mandate*—a requirement that everyone buy insurance. The legality of the individual mandate went before the Supreme Court in the United States in 2012 and was approved by a very thin margin. Most other developed countries, including Canada, Britain, Switzerland, the Netherlands, Australia, and Japan, solve the adverse selection problem in health insurance with either a mandate or a nationalized health-care system.

While the adverse selection problem in health care has been studied and considered at great length, companies in other industries sometimes fall victim to adverse selection of customers simply because they don't do their research. Here's an example that I can relate to because—in addition to working very hard on my search for a life partner—I am shamelessly and constantly in search of higher frequent-flier status. The desire for a wonderful woman to tell me she loves me is my most important goal right now, but not far behind is my quest for United Airlines' 1K credentials.

Consider Ryan Bingham, George Clooney's character in *Up in the Air*, who flies over 10 million miles on American Airlines. To reward his loyalty, the airline provides him with untold attention and perks. A few Bingham-like people exist in real life, and the airlines make it a top priority to keep them happy so that they remain loyal customers.

In 1981, American Airlines introduced the AAirpass (for real—we're no longer talking about the movie). For $250,000, a customer could buy unlimited first-class travel on the airline for life. For an additional $150,000, she could bring a companion on any flight she took. Now, that is a lot of money. I fly a lot, but it would take a long time before I spent a quarter of a million dollars on airfare. But to the Ryan Binghams of the world, it isn't that hard to run through a few hundred thousand dollars of tickets. So, while most of us didn't buy an AAirpass, people like Ryan Bingham did, and saved a substantial amount of money doing so.

Bob Crandall, who was American's CEO for much of the life of the AAirpass, admitted, "We thought originally it would be something that firms would buy for top employees. It soon became apparent that the public was smarter than we were." Aha—hidden information! Remember, that's what leads to adverse selection. Some AAirpass holders have been known to fly so much in *one month* that buying the tickets would have cost $125,000. Having learned its lesson the hard way, American steadily raised the price of AAirpass to over $1 million before canceling it altogether. Recently, American has been investigating some AAirpass holders in hopes that it can show the customers acted fraudulently, thus giving the airline an excuse to cancel its obligation.

Adverse selection of customers can also be costly for any company that loans money to people. Credit scores, financial information, and the like are very helpful for banks and credit card companies that want to separate good credit risks from bad credit risks. However, assessing people's credit is an imperfect process, as evidenced by the fact that about 5 percent of credit card debt and car loans are never repaid.

You may know Capital One as the company with the silly Viking advertisements. But the story of Capital One, now a huge credit card company, began as a lesson in using adverse selection to one's own advantage. Capital One was founded in 1988, when Richard Fairbank convinced a small regional bank to experiment with its credit card unit. At that time, pretty much all credit cards issued in the United States had the same interest rate on unpaid balances. Annual fees were comparable across cards. Fairbank believed that he could figure out ways to draw in new and riskier customers at higher interest rates while charging lower interest rates to safer customers, generating higher profits.

Initially, it didn't work out. Capital One tried to advertise various unique features of their credit card, such as teaser rates. Most of the customers they attracted were unappealing—they either did not run balances (which made them unprofitable) or they defaulted. Capital One was on the verge of shutting down when one of Fairbank's experiments struck adverse-selection gold. In essence, Fairbank created the credit card equivalent of a new online dating site that took all the non-losers away from Match.com while leaving all the losers behind.

The bank began to offer very attractive interest rates to any new customer who transferred his credit card balance on a competitor's credit card to Capital One. That is, Capital One would pay off the person's credit card debt and the person would now owe Capital One that debt at a lower "teaser" interest rate. Capital One would charge the person little to no interest for the first year after the balance transfer and then increase to the market interest rate. Such balance transfers are now a standard offering in the current credit card market, but they were unheard of in 1988.

One important thing to know about the credit card industry is that the most profitable customers are those who carry balances and do not default. Balance transfers, at least in 1988, appealed to credit card customers who had both of these attributes. A customer would obviously not have a balance to transfer if she did not carry one on her credit card, and one who did not plan to repay the balance wouldn't bother transferring that balance to a card with a more attractive interest rate. Thus, customers who paid their balance in full every month and those who were likely to default did not find Capital One's balance transfers attractive. But those customers are unprofitable and the other banks were stuck with them in the adverse selection process.

Balance transfers were a boon to Capital One, and they were just the first of many profitable innovations in credit card marketing that have made the company a huge success. However, the company's current success no longer rests on balance transfers because, it turns out, balance transfers are only highly profitable when other credit card companies don't offer them. Over time (and you would be surprised how long it took), other credit card companies started copying Capital One's new idea. Eventually, most credit card holders with even marginally decent credit had their choice of multiple balance transfer offers. In fact, the tables eventually turned, in that balance transfers created their own adverse selection problem for the banks that offered them. This is because very savvy credit card customers can transfer their balance to a new card every year and never pay any interest. These customers are essentially getting interest-free loans from the credit card companies that offer balance transfers.

Buffet Restaurants Attract a Certain Type of Diner

Do you ever go to an all-you-can-eat buffet? Ever notice something about the other patrons? The principle of adverse selection suggests that people who go to all-you-can-eat buffets, where everyone pays the same price, are unlikely to be a random selection of the population. They are likely to be, putting it as gently as possible, "gravity challenged." Or you might say they are, using an online dating term, "voluptuous." If a buffet costs the same amount for all customers, only those customers with big appetites get their money's worth, and that trait is typically reflected in the size of the patrons.

Note, however, that there are two reasons people eat very large amounts of food at buffets. The first is the adverse selection problem I just described—patrons have hidden information about their appetites that they reveal when they determine whether the buffet is worth its price. But the second reason is a key concept that economists refer to as *moral hazard*.

Moral hazard refers to *hidden action* rather than *hidden information*; it is really just a fancy term that means that people respond to incentives. While the customers at a buffet are typically more rotund than those you might find at other restaurants, they also share another trait—they eat more when dining at buffets than they eat when they go to other restaurants. At an all-you-can-eat restaurant, diners have no reason to stop eating as long as they are enjoying what they eat. It costs nothing to have another serving of chicken, salad, or dessert. So, as long as you are not *really* full, you go ahead and eat some more. At a standard restaurant, you order more food only if you think it will be worth the extra money. You have an incentive to stop eating sooner because it costs money to keep going.

Moral hazard issues are everywhere, and they often are coupled with adverse selection. Together, moral hazard and adverse selection are the key examples of what economists call *agency* problems—where one economic agent can take an action that affects others. I am taking a detour to discuss moral hazard and contrast it with adverse selection. But I'm afraid moral hazard does not get its own chapter in this book. That's not because it doesn't deserve it but rather because there just isn't much moral hazard in online dating. It is simply one important economics concept that does not fit my theme.

Adverse Selection Can Be Tempered through Incentive Pay

While there is really no way to avoid adverse selection on dating sites, some companies have found that they can use money to solve the adverse selection problem in the job market. You may have seen this strategy in action, without knowing it, if you've ever cracked your car windshield. If you have, there's a good chance you called Safelite Auto

Glass—they have an army of auto glass installers who drive a truck out to your house and replace it.

A while back, Safelite was doing OK, but its managers thought it could do better. The glass installers were paid an hourly rate and, though they could be fired if they were negligent, they had no incentive to use their time wisely. The company decided to try a pay-for-performance scheme where glass installers would be paid about $10 for each windshield they installed (as long as that was more than their old hourly rate). They also implemented measures to insure the installers did not increase their output by doing a shoddy job.

My colleague Edward Lazear studied data on productivity at Safelite before and after they changed the pay structure. The new pay plan was implemented at different times in different locations, which allowed Lazear to see the same installers on both pay plans while controlling for other factors.

The study showed that productivity went up by 40 percent when Safelite switched from hourly pay to pay-per-windshield. Half of the increase in productivity came from the fact that windshield installers were more productive than they had been before. That is, the incentive worked and increased a typical installer's productivity by 20 percent. This improvement shows that Safelite had been facing a substantial moral hazard or hidden action problem when paying by the hour. Installers were doing their work more slowly than they could have been doing it.

But a careful look at the data showed that the increased productivity was not only a result of better incentives motivating employees to work harder. The other half of the increase in productivity came from fixing an adverse selection problem.

The new pay-for-performance plan meant that better installers would get paid more than slower installers. The change made the job more attractive to more-talented installers and made the job less attractive to less-talented installers. Overall, more good installers sought work at Safelite while many of the less-productive installers left Safelite for slower-paced alternatives. The pay plan forced potential glass installers to reveal their private information about their talent, work ethic, and overall productivity.

Performance pay and all-you-can-eat buffets both illustrate the coexistence of moral hazard and adverse selection problems quite well. But maybe my personal favorite example of how these two forces exist side by side is Volvo drivers. When you think of Volvo drivers, you probably think of soccer Moms and suburban families obsessed with safety. The company's cars have always been on the safety frontier and, as a result, the cars are often purchased by safety-conscious families.

But Volvos are also attractive to another group—bad drivers. If you know that you are an unsafe driver who is more likely to get into an accident, what kind of car would you drive? A Hummer, perhaps, but a Volvo would also be a good choice. "Volvo driver" has become an insult for a bad driver in some circles, with the online *Urban Dictonary* definition starting, "Someone who is so bad at driving that they want a car that is perceived overly safe. They drive slowly in the fast lane, they cut into traffic causing other drivers to swerve and brake violently to avoid a collision." People who have private information that they are unsafe drivers reveal this private information through their choice to protect themselves with a Volvo.

The moral hazard or hidden action aspect of owning a Volvo comes from the fact that, once you own one, you feel empowered to take more chances on the road. One blogger summed this phenomenon up, writing, "Even the best drivers seem to deteriorate once you put them in a Volvo." For some reason, Volvo drivers in Australia have an especially bad reputation for driving with no regard for others on the road, leading the company to fight back (ironically) with what was known as the "Bloody Volvo Driver" advertising campaign.

I have not seen any actual scientific evidence that Volvo drivers are systematically more erratic than drivers of other cars. But you might want to get out of the way if you see a Volvo on the road, just to be safe. On the other hand, you no longer need to avoid people who try to find their next mate through online dating. We're not *all* lemons—or even Volvos—anymore.

Some Things to Take Away from Chapter 7

A Key Insight from Economics: There are some markets where only owners and producers of low-quality goods have an incentive to sell. Those with high-quality goods stay out of the market.

A Valuable or Important Empirical Finding by Economists Who Study Adverse Selection: When companies base pay on people's output, they attract more-productive people and their less-productive employees are more likely to leave.

When It Comes to Adverse Selection, Dating Is a Lot Like: Buying a used car, going to an all-you-can-eat restaurant, choosing a credit card.

Dating Advice: If someone has been active on a dating site for a long time, stay away.

8

POSITIVE ASSORTATIVE MATING

Why Everyone in the Office and the Neighborhood Is Similar

I am a terrible dancer. I have no natural rhythm, I move in an ungraceful manner, and my lack of talent is compounded by pronounced self-consciousness when I'm on the dance floor. If dancing were a primary issue in making couples happy together, it would be bad for me to date a woman who was a good dancer. She would be very frustrated by my reluctance to dance, my inability to keep up with her while dancing, and with having to watch me try. So it would make much more sense for good dancers to date one another and for women who cannot dance to go out with the likes of me.

The top law firms recruit the cream of the crop from the top law schools. Many other firms employ the merely excellent.

There are plenty of prestigious law firms that recruit new lawyers from good law schools and that are quite picky about whom they select. But there are a few firms that will, with rare exceptions, make offers only to the top students (those who make the law review or earn—and I am not making this up, this is considered an honor among lawyers—"Order of the Coif") at the most elite law schools. These firms, such as Wachtell, Lipton, Rosen, and Katz and Cravath, Swaine and Moore, do some of the most important and complicated legal work in the business and financial world. They believe that they need the very best and brightest lawyers in order to do such work effectively. The fact that clients demand these firms' services indicates that their business model is sensible. In the market for lawyers, then, the best and the brightest lawyers are matched to the best and most valued firms just as I would date women who cannot dance in a world where dancing was key to matchmaking.

Why do dancers and lawyers pair off this way? This is a pretty intuitive idea, but some economist somewhere—borrowing from the biologists who use it to explain the same phenomenon in the animal kingdom—gave it a completely ridiculous and unintuitive name (which does not even pass spell checkers): *positive assortative mating* or *positive assortative matching*. We'll use the former here, but you're free to choose your favorite. The basic idea is that people sort into partnerships or groups in a manner that is non-random and, in particular, can be "ordered." So in the strictest version of positive assortative mating, the "best" woman would be mated to the "best" man, the second-best to the second-best, and so on.

When we see positive assortative mating, it will generally be the case that it leads to a "better" outcome than if people (or lawyers and firms) matched randomly. Consider the following simple example (where, as I'll explain in a moment, the names are purposely chosen to be androgynous). Suppose that Addison is a very beautiful woman and Chris is homely. Now suppose that Bailey is an extremely handsome and well-built man while Devon is pasty, totally out of shape, and generally unattractive. Other things being equal, both men would probably like to date Addison and both women would choose Bailey. However, the best way to maximize overall utility is probably to pair Addison with Bailey and Chris with Devon. Addison and Bailey would be able to enjoy one another's company with less insecurity, for example.

Positive assortative mating is clearly an important force in the dating market. More attractive and more wealthy people are always more in demand (as discussed in the next chapter), but demand for attractive people on dating sites is especially high among other attractive people. More broadly, researchers have shown that there is strong positive assortative mating in terms of physical attractiveness, income, race, education, and other traits on dating sites.

Things do not have to work that way, however. There are cases, as we will discuss, where *negative assortative mating* (matching Addison and Devon) or *random mating* (matching Addison randomly to either Devon or Bailey) make more sense. These alternative scenarios would happen in any setting where the best partner in a match (that is, the *maximum quality* within the match) is all that matters for happiness. So suppose there is a swank, exciting nightclub that admits only attractive people and their dates. Then, if all they cared about was entering this nightclub, Addison, Bailey, Chris, and Devon would be best off as a group with negative assortative mating where Addison and Devon are one couple and Bailey and Chris are another couple. Then they could all get into the nightclub and increase their total utility.[1]

Throughout this chapter, we will come back to Addison, Bailey, Chris, and Devon regularly. Sometimes they will be people looking for dates or a spouse, other times they will be employees looking for a job, and so forth. In each case, they can be categorized in some dimension. Sometimes I will order or rank them from highest to lowest and, to keep it intuitive, the ranking will always be alphabetical. Addison will be the "best" (or Addison and Bailey will be the top) and Devon the "worst" (or Chris and Devon will be the bottom). Other times, the order will not be any sort of ranking but just categorization. For example, Addison and Bailey might be female, a racial minority, or gay while Chris and Devon are male, Caucasian, or heterosexual. Their names were specifically chosen to be androgynous (these names all rank reasonably high on baby name lists for both genders in the United States) to allow for same-sex or opposite-sex pairings, depending on the context. For the rest of this chapter, we will look at several examples and ask: When do we see Addison pairing with Bailey? When do we see Addison

---

1. Remember that I'm talking here about which groups are actual couples in a relationship. I'm not advocating swapping, though I realize that may be best for a different kind of exclusive nightclub than the one I am imagining here.

pairing with Devon? And, Why might these pairings make sense? In the case of dancing (where the people are ordered by dance ability) or law coworkers (where they are ordered by lawyer skills), we have already seen that the Addisons of the world typically pair off with the Baileys. That pattern holds in many other contexts, but not all.

Mating in College and Its Long-Term Consequences

Colleges are a great alternative to online dating—lots of available people are around and they have many opportunities to get to know one another. In fact, when I was in college, the school's president would frequently remind the student body that there was a very good chance we were going to school with our future spouse. Many couples meet in college, so it should be no great surprise that you are much more likely to marry a college graduate if you went to college than if you did not. For example, consider all American married couples in the year 2000 where the wife is between the ages of eighteen and forty. A little more than one-quarter of the people in these marriages were college graduates. But two-thirds of the spouses of college graduates were college graduates. Similarly, about 11 percent of the people in these marriages had not completed high school, but more than half of those who had not completed high school were married to another high school dropout. So, if we were to rank our four friends by their education (that is, Addison stayed in school the longest, Devon the shortest), we would be very likely to find Addison married to Bailey and Chris to Devon.

This pattern of "like mates with like" is much broader than traditional marriages and education, however. Gay couples, lesbian couples, and opposite-sex unmarried cohabitating couples are equally similar in terms of education as are married couples. Partners in all types of committed relationships are also more similar than a random match in terms of income. People who work relatively long hours and make relatively more money live with other people who work hard and earn high incomes. "Power couples" are fairly common because people with high earning power pair off, leaving the less-well-off to each other.

Power couples are especially common among unmarried long-term couples. That is, both members of a couple are more likely to be high earners among unmarried and same-sex domestic partnerships than they are among married couples. Incomes and hours worked are more similar within same-sex and unmarried couples than within married couples. This data suggests that married couples are more likely than the other types of couples to follow traditional specialized roles where one member of the couple earns the money and the other takes care of household tasks and child care.

These subtle differences between married and unmarried couples are small, though, compared with the fact that positive assortative mating is very strong in couples of all kinds. The authors of one study conclude that, "We find evidence of positive assortative mating for all traits and across all types of couples." So, *no matter what characteristic is used* to rank the four, we expect to see Addison married to or in a relationship with Bailey and Chris attached to Devon.

Well, actually, it is not quite true that there is positive assortative mating for *all* traits. Negative assortative mating better describes sorting by gender. The majority of people are heterosexual, so most people match with opposites on at least this one trait.

Positive Assortative Mating Makes It Hard to Move Up

In the movie *Pretty Woman*, Richard Gere plays a wealthy businessman and Julia Roberts portrays a call girl who has had a rough life. They fall in love and live happily ever after, allowing Roberts's character to climb the social hierarchy. Though a bit unconventional, it is the type of rags-to-riches story people love to hear and Hollywood loves to provide. But how realistic is it? People do move up and down the economic ladder, but not as much as you might think. One big obstacle holding people back is positive assortative mating—very few hookers marry rich men. We tend to pair off within the social class we grew up in, which reinforces our positions in the economic system.

Just as couples tend to have similar education, couples typically come from similar backgrounds. So not only is it the case that a person with a college education is more likely to have a partner with a college education, but the children of people with college educations are more likely to have partners whose parents have a college education. The similarity of parents' education and other characteristics among married couples has grown over time, which is probably making the *Pretty Woman* scenario even less likely.

At least in the United States and the United Kingdom, this trend may be making it more difficult to move up the economic ladder. In the US and the UK, relative to other developed countries, it has always been unlikely that a poor child would grow up to be wealthy. In recent decades in both countries, the rich have gotten richer while the poor have gotten poorer. This shift may have also helped make it harder to move from poor to rich. In countries where the differences in incomes between rich and poor are not as great, such as in Scandinavia, there has always been more movement up and down the social ladder between generations.

Whatever the trend, it's very hard to move up the economic ladder in most countries. And it appears that an important contributing factor to this quagmire is that we pair off with people who are more and more like we are, both in terms of family backgrounds and personal characteristics.

We Work with People Like Ourselves

On dating sites, the people who are most like you are the ones most interested in your profile. You meet people similar to you in school and through your parents. So where are you going to meet people who are different from you? How about work? Lots of couples meet in the office (for one piece of hard data, there were three workplace weddings in *The Office*'s nine-year run). Maybe work is a good place to meet someone different and broaden your horizons.

No such luck. Workplaces are another bastion of positive assortative mating. We work with people who are like us because different kinds of employers appeal to different types of workers.

There is positive assortative mating in the labor market, in that the most productive workers match with the firms that can use their skills most productively. Most notably, large firms pay their workers more than small firms do. This is not a new development—Henry Moore did a study of Italian women in the textile industry one hundred years ago and found that women at plants with more than five hundred workers made about 40 percent more than women in plants with under twenty workers. Moore went further than to just note the extra pay, stating, "… as the size of the establishment increases, the condition of the laborer improves in all directions—his wages rise, he is employed a greater number of days in a year, his employment varies less from month to month, and his hours of labor, per day, decrease." (A hundred years ago, even if a person studied women, he felt compelled to masculinize anyone with a job.)

In the century since Moore went to Italy, many studies have found the same basic idea in many different work settings around the world. In Japan in 1988, for example, a woman working at a company with over a thousand employees made an average of ¥1,554 per hour, while a woman at a company with more than a hundred but under a thousand employees made ¥1,105 per hour. The women at the bigger company had also worked there longer and attained a bit more education.

In the United States in 1993, the average man at a company with over a thousand employees made 11 percent more than a man at a company with one hundred to five hundred workers. Some of this discrepancy can be explained by other factors—people at bigger firms tend to stay at the same company longer, have a bit more education, and they are much more likely to belong to a union and work full-time. But these figures are also an understatement of the extra pay from working at a large firm. Fringe benefits are generally more generous at large firms.

It is incontrovertible that there is a strong and nearly universal relationship between firm size and wages; but why? There are surely a number of contributing factors, several of which have nothing to do with positive assortative mating. That is, there are several good reasons that a person would receive a higher wage from a large employer than that same person would from a smaller company. One contributing factor is that it is harder to keep track of and monitor workers at large firms. By paying their employees more, large employers give them an incentive not to shirk. Another possible explanation is that working at big companies might simply be less fun—think *Dilbert*—so people have to be paid a premium to be willing to work there rather than in a more enjoyable work environment.

Furthermore, it's possible that big firms simply have deeper pockets and either cannot or do not find it worth the trouble to bargain as hard. We might expect this notion to be true simply because of who does the bargaining. If I work at a big company and go in in to ask for a raise, it does not come out of my boss's own pocket. At smaller firms, the wage rates are likely to be set by the owner or at least someone with a bigger stake in the company who has strong incentives to guard expenses closely.

But while those explanations are important and surely a part of the firm size/wage relationship, positive assortative mating is also a major driver of the firm-size premium. The types of people who work at big firms are the types of people who would make more money wherever they work. As noted in the Japanese and US data above, people at large companies are more educated and have more work experience. Many studies have also shown that people who work at larger firms are simply "better" (more productive) workers, holding other characteristics constant. That is, big employers are able to attract employees who would be more productive than the typical worker, no matter where they worked. For example, one detailed and careful analysis of half a million French firms found that most of the difference in wages between big and small firms can be explained by the fact that "better" workers work at larger firms, even holding constant such characteristics as education and labor market experience. Other researchers looking at other countries have reached similar conclusions.

We can safely conclude that there is positive assortative mating between workers and firms in the sense that more skilled workers go to bigger firms. Put another way, suppose Addison is the most educated, the hardest working, or simply the smartest one of our four friends and we rank the others the usual way. Our best guess would be that we would find Addison working for a *Fortune* 500 company, Bailey at a medium-sized regional business with maybe a thousand employees, Chris at a small company with twenty people, and Devon as a sole proprietor operating out of his house. Remember, however, that these are only averages, and that firm size is not the only factor determining productivity. There are, of course, plenty of very productive people at small companies and many unproductive people working at big companies.

But why, on average, do more-skilled people work at bigger companies? One argument is that it makes sense to have more-productive people in places where their characteristics can rub off on more people. In other words, a really good boss can make the people who work for her better, so it makes sense to have more people working for better bosses. But that logic suggests only that big firms should have good bosses, not that all workers at big firms should be better. But if many of the employees at bigger firms have the potential to move up the ladder one day, we would expect people at all levels of bigger firms to be more productive. That is, we want Addison to work at a company with a lot of other Addisons whom she can mold into productive employees.

Big firms have the potential to use employees' skills more productively for other reasons, though. For example, they can buy the best capital equipment and the nicest computers or they can move people around to keep them busy. In that case, we want the most productive people at these firms because the extra productivity effect of combining good workers and good firms is multiplicative. Consider this very simple example. Suppose a big grocery chain has a piece of equipment that makes sandwiches. If Addison is running the machine, it will make 200 sandwiches per hour, but if Bailey runs the machine, it will only make 150. Now suppose that there is a local deli, and Addison can make 20 sandwiches per hour working behind the counter. Bailey would only make 15 at the same deli. Addison has the same relative output in each place—she's always one-third more productive than Bailey. But if Addison has the job at the chain while Bailey works at the local deli, they make a total of 215 sandwiches per hour. If they swap places, their total productivity decreases to 170.

What Makes a Good Team at the Office?

By now, you have noticed a common thread here. When choosing who dates whom, who marries whom, or who works with whom, we tend to see positive assortative mating—the good-looking, the rich, and the highly educated pair off with one another, leaving the less attractive, less well off, and less educated to form their own group. In almost every possible situation, you will find these same results—the Addisons and Baileys of the world are more likely to be together, with the Chrises and the Devons off in another group.

So Addison and Bailey (the productive or skilled people) are more likely to work at big firms than Chris and Devon. But what about within a company? Let's move all four into the same company and form workplace teams to make them as productive as possible. Suppose we need two teams of two to do some task at our company. Should we have Addison work with Bailey so the stars are together, or should we put Addison with Devon so the star can rub off on the dud? It turns out that this case will often provide the exception to the theme we've seen throughout this chapter. While positive assortative mating is common and seemingly appropriate in determining dating outcomes, relationships, and where people work, there are many workplaces where productivity is highest when we put Addison and Devon on one team and Bailey and Chris on another. This phenomenon likely has an interesting but not very economics-oriented explanation: guilt and shame.

Barton Hamilton, Jack Nickerson, and Hideo Owan studied output at a garment factory in California that switched from paying each worker a piece rate for each sewing task to paying teams of workers a set amount for each final garment the team produced. They found that people are more productive in teams (these were small teams of six or seven people); total output in the plant went up 18 percent. They also found that the ideal pairing was negative assortative mating—that is, the best way to form teams was to pair Addison with Devon and Bailey with Chris. Working with high-output partners shamed the lazy people into working harder more than working with the lazy people made the hard workers slack off. That is, everyone worked just a little bit less when paired with Devon (the slow one) and a bit more when paired with Addison (the sewing whiz), but the "I have to keep up with Addison" effect was stronger.

Economists Armin Falk and Andrea Ichino found exactly the same thing in another study. They set up an operation in which they recruited high school students from around Zurich to stuff envelopes with a survey distributed by the University of Zurich. They wanted to know whether a given worker would stuff more envelopes working by herself or in a room with another envelope stuffer. They had three main findings. First, people stuffed more envelopes when working with others than when working alone. Second, while working in pairs could make people more productive by alleviating boredom, it appears that the stuffers actually cared what the other person thought—there was a clear pattern whereby both stuffers would either work hard or have low output.

Rarely did one stuffer have much higher productivity than the other. Finally, Falk and Ichino found the exact same team composition effects as in the garment factory—output was higher when the working groups were Addison and Devon on one team and Bailey and Chris on the other than when Addison paired with Bailey and Chris paired with Devon. Apparently, guilt is very powerful in the workplace.

In yet another study along these lines, Alex Mas and Enrico Moretti pored over a supermarket chain's checkout records. To understand their research's setup, imagine the checkout area of a typical grocery store. The registers are all in a line, and the workers who scan the groceries through the checkout system are lined up so that they can see the backs of the checkers in one direction but cannot see checkers in the other direction at all. So, a checker can watch anywhere from zero to several people do their job in front of him, and be watched by zero to several people doing theirs behind him.

At the chain of stores in question, there were typically seven or so checkers working at any given time. The checkers would each start their shifts, stop their shifts, and go on break at different and almost random times. Mas and Moretti found several interesting patterns in the checkers' data. First, anytime a very productive checker (that is, an Addison) started her shift, the productivity of all the other checkers went up by a little bit. Anytime Devon started, the productivity of the other checkers went down a bit. Mas and Moretti then went on to show that cashiers should be teamed using negative assortative mating—Devon should work when Addison is on duty and Bailey should work when Chris does. To put those results in perspective, suppose Devon and Bailey are already working when Addison starts her shift. Devon starts checking about 2 percent more groceries through when Addison starts, while Bailey increases his grocery throughput by roughly 0.5 percent.

Perhaps the most interesting thing Mas and Moretti found, however, is that Addison can increase other checkers' output only if she is put in a position where she can clearly see the lower-performing checkers. The shame of Addison seeing him work slowly provides an incentive for Devon to step up his game. If Devon can see Addison working hard, but Addison's back is turned to Devon so that she does not see the slow worker, Devon does not respond. Seeing Addison working hard does not motivate Devon, but the fear that Addison will see him working slowly gets Devon to step it up. So, at least in the case of supermarket checkers, negative assortative mating is optimal, but only if you let the stars watch the slugs.

When Should We Start Grouping People?

Supermarket checkers and envelope stuffers may be best teamed using negative assortative mating, but their cases are really exceptions—we see positive assortative mating almost everywhere. As noted back at the beginning of the chapter, lawyers are "mated" positively. The so-called best and the brightest work together at the elite "white-shoe" firms. These people went to law school together at Yale and Harvard, where they worked with each other on the law review. Before that, many of them also went to top undergraduate schools with other extremely smart and accomplished people. In fact, we "track" people in academics from an even younger age.

One example of this tracking is the selection of five math "lanes" in my children's high school. The school puts the best math students together in a group and separates them out from the other students. So, if Addison and her friends are high school students and we rank them by innate math ability, my kids' high school (and most of its peer institutions) believes in positive assortative mating. They set up classes where Addison and Bailey are in one class while Chris and Devon are in another. It's not just math, of course. By senior year, many of the students are taking only Advanced Placement classes, while others are not taking any. At this point, Addison and Bailey see each other regularly in a variety of classes (and compare notes on how their applications to Princeton are going), while Chris and Devon also have plenty of classes together but rarely see the other two.

The main reason for this sorting is fairly obvious and is completely different from why we see positive assortative mating on dating sites. On dating sites, we pair off on the basis of who we want to spend time with. But in choosing classrooms, we group kids so that they will learn the most as a collective. If we put Devon and Addison in the same math class, the teacher would either have to go so slowly for Devon's sake that Addison's learning would be impeded, or move the material along quickly enough to keep Addison engaged and lose Devon in the process. The total amount of learning is greatest when Devon and Chris are in the same class and Addison and Bailey are in a different class.

But this arrangement comes at a cost to Chris and Devon. Just as supermarket checkers are influenced by their peers, so are students. The magnitude varies substantially depending on where or when you look, but economists and other social scientists have generally shown there are important "peer effects" in schools. If Addison is added to the group of students in a class, everyone learns a little more; if Devon is added, everyone learns a little less. The overall level of achievement across the whole class is highest when Addison is in a class with other high achievers, but Devon pays at least a small price for being excluded. Positive assortative mating in the form of classroom tracking may be optimal, but it is yet another factor that makes moving up the socioeconomic ladder increasingly difficult.

For better or worse, fair or unfair, the world is full of positive assortative mating. We see it on Match.com and anywhere couples are forming, but we see it just about everywhere else, too. People like to live with, go to school with, and work with people like themselves and they are generally more productive when they do (at least across certain dimensions). We may wish our inclinations were otherwise, but we are fighting nature. Our colleagues in the physical sciences have shown that Red Crossbills (birds), Icelandic Threespine Sticklebacks (fish), and Water Striders (bugs) show positive assortative mating by bill and body size. Why should we humans be any different?

Some Things to Take Away from Chapter 8

A Key Insight from Economics: People form groups in many different contexts (family, home, neighborhood) in such a way that the people in the groups are much more similar to each other than they are to people not in the group.

A Valuable or Important Empirical Finding by Economists Who Study Positive Assortative Mating: In a lot of workplace settings, it makes sense to have the most productive people work with the least productive people. The stars make the slugs better, and the slugs don't slow the stars down much.

When It Comes to Positive Assortative Mating, Dating Is a Lot Like: Dancing, assigning shifts at the supermarket, sorting kids into math classes.

Dating Advice: You are going to end up with someone a lot like yourself, so accept that and move on with your life.

9

THE RETURNS TO SKILLS

Education and Good Looks Pay

Taste in mates differs, of course, but there are some characteristics that inarguably make a person a better catch. Looks and money come to mind immediately. We spend a lot of time with our mates, and they might as well be easy on the eyes and/or able to help us go on exotic vacations, buy a nice house, and reach other material goals. I will admit that—all else being equal—the better looking and richer my partner, the happier I expect to be.

The importance of good looks and money in the dating market has been documented by, among others, Gunter Hitsch, Ali Hortacsu, and Dan Ariely. They looked at over twenty-two thousand online daters located in Boston and San Diego. The results found, pretty simply, that men are looking for attractive women, and women are looking for attractive and rich men. Sure, there are other attributes that matter, but looks and money are the big draws. Of course, in order to determine the effects of looks, the authors of the study had to determine who was good-looking, which is typically accomplished by paying undergraduates to look at pictures of people and rate them on a numerical scale.[1] Ratings by multiple students are generally highly correlated in these kinds of studies, indicating it is possible to rate "attractiveness" fairly objectively.

So how much does it help to be good-looking on a dating site? As you might expect, a lot. Looks are the single best predictor of how often someone on a dating site will be contacted by interested fellow daters. People in the most attractive 10 percent receive about twice as many e-mails as people who are average looking. An average-looking person, in turn, gets about twice as many e-mails as someone who is among the least-attractive 10 percent on the site. Hitsch and his coauthors also identified an interesting "superstar effect" for men only. The "hottest" 5 percent of men get twice as many e-mails as men who are in the sixth through tenth percentile.

The dating site OkCupid has done its own analysis of the relationship between attractiveness and how many messages people receive. The site's blog states that "a hot woman receives roughly 4x the messages an average-looking woman gets, and 25x as many as an ugly one."

---

1. In the case of the Boston and San Diego online daters, the ratings were done by University of Chicago undergraduates. I was tempted to make sarcastic comments about University of Chicago students' inability to know what an attractive person is but, according to the online dating site DateMySchool.com, the school's "hotness ratio" is quite respectable—just behind UCLA and cheerleader-heavy University of Oklahoma.

While general hotness matters, other more specific physical attributes are also important. Tall men get contacted more often, while medium-height women do better than both tall and short women. Overweight people are contacted less often, even beyond any effect of weight on their attractiveness rating. Finally, as we have all been led to believe would be the case, blonde women get contacted more often (though the effect is quite small). Blondes may or may not actually be more fun, but they are proven to be slightly more popular.

Looks matter a lot, but they are not all that matters—well, at least not to women. A man who makes $250,000 per year, holding other things equal, gets contacted two and a half times as often as a man who makes under $50,000. Men care less about income—women who make more do not get appreciably more e-mails than lower-income women.

Hitch and his colleagues found a few other things that matter a little bit in attracting mates, but nothing in the same league as looks and money. More education makes a man a bit more attractive on the dating site, but has no effect for women. Women are more attracted to lawyers, doctors, men in the military, and, stereotypically, firefighters. (They do not mention economists, but that's surely because the sample size is too small.) Men, on the other hand, do not care at all what a woman's profession is. Apparently, it's true—men are pigs and care only about looks.

The attributes that make people attractive on dating sites in Boston and San Diego are, unsurprisingly, pretty much the same ones that make them attractive in Korea. Soohyung Lee followed couples from their first contact on a Korean dating site through their decision to become engaged, allowing her to more explicitly measure what people are looking for in a spouse rather than in a date. She finds, again, that men are much more interested in looks than any other characteristic, while women care about looks, money, and a few other things. For example, a typical Korean woman is equally drawn to a man with an exceptionally attractive face and an average-looking man who makes an extra $44,000 per year. A typical man, however, will prefer an average-looking woman to an extremely attractive alternative only if the average-looking woman makes at least $150,000 extra per year. In other words, men are willing to "pay" about three times as much as women for beauty in their mates.

So, though it's probably not a big surprise to you, "hot" people get asked on more dates and rich men are more attractive to women. There are no formal studies of what makes people attractive on same-sex dating sites but, anecdotally, it appears to be very similar to heterosexual dating sites. Looks and income (or at least employment) matter.

These findings—that people care about looks and money—have often been related to evolutionary psychology and evolutionary biology, but you may be wondering what any of this has to do with economics. Well, there are two answers.

First, the preferences for money, attractiveness, and other features in a mate are simply another area in which we see people's utility functions, as discussed in chapter 1. Remember that *utility* is just another way to say *happiness*, and we make decisions that we think will increase our happiness. From the studies of the online dating market, we can infer that men are happier when they are with more attractive women and women are happier when they are with richer, more attractive men.

Second, as this chapter will examine in more detail, people are born with or acquire certain attributes. Some people are particularly smart, some people are particularly good-looking, some people are particularly athletic, and so forth. In marketplaces, these attributes have value—they can be exchanged. In the dating market, I can get dates with women who are attracted to middle-aged men with a lot of education, a good (if not great) income, and devilishly good looks (I'm editorializing a bit there). Now let's think about how these and other attributes affect someone's status in the labor market.

It Pays to Be Attractive

Dan Hamermesh is an economist at the University of Texas who has done a lot of important work in labor economics. But what he's best known for beyond the walls of academia are his studies of the connection between looks and income. Back in 1994 Hamermesh and Jeff Biddle undertook the first economic study to carefully explore the relationship between attractiveness and income. Using a number of 1970s surveys from the United States and Canada that included measures of people's attractiveness, they found that a typical person with "below average" looks made 10 to 15 percent less than an average-looking person with similar skills. A typical person with "above average" looks, on the other hand, made 5 to 10 percent more than an average-looking person. Men are penalized a bit more for being unattractive relative to women, and men are also rewarded less for being attractive. That is, women get a bigger premium for being hot and a smaller penalty for being unattractive.

You might think that overweight people would suffer a fate similar to unattractive people. But Hamermesh and others have generally found that weight is not closely related to income for most groups when attractiveness is held constant. One study, which had a particularly large sample (no pun intended) and very good measures of weight, found that white women who are fifty pounds overweight make about 8 percent less than "height-weight appropriate" white women but that no other gender and ethnic group suffers an obesity penalty in the labor market.

Note that the findings regarding beauty and body size line up exactly with those from the dating market. Good looks are rewarded, and weight does not carry much penalty once you adjust for looks. But while it was easy to understand why more-attractive people get more attention on dating sites, it is not as obvious why attractiveness is a valuable asset in the labor market. Hamermesh and others have spent a great deal of time trying to determine why beauty pays.

One possibility is that good looks are productive—they make people more valuable to their employers. This effect is obviously important for actors and, to some extent, athletes (the good-looking ones get more endorsements) and politicians. But being attractive should not, for example, make a person a better lawyer (except maybe on a TV legal drama, where all the lawyers just happen to be model material). Or should it?

Biddle and Hamermesh got hold of the yearbooks from a large, prestigious law school for a number of years in the 1970s and 1980s, and matched students' pictures to information the school collected in later alumni surveys. The study is focused on men's looks because there were not enough female lawyers at the time to generate precise estimates. Biddle and Hamermesh found that more-attractive lawyers made more money than less-attractive lawyers, and that this effect grew over time. So there was very little extra pay for the more attractive upon graduating from law school, but there was a substantial handsomeness premium five years after graduation and an even bigger premium fifteen years after graduation. Two ways this premium likely develops over time are that more-attractive lawyers are better at generating business (that is, those in need of legal help prefer to give their business to attractive lawyers), and that they are more likely to get promoted to be a partner in a law firm, independent of legal skill.

Now, if you took any statistics or social science classes in college, I know what you're thinking. Correlation does not equal causation. There could well be reasons that more-attractive people make more money other than the possibility that being attractive directly leads to making more money. For example, maybe very diligent and ambitious people, in addition to doing what it takes to be successful in their careers, are also good at grooming themselves and staying fit. Then these people would be rich and attractive, but only because of some other unrelated factor. Alternatively, the causality could go the other way. Maybe people who make a lot of money can make themselves more attractive. Plastic surgery, tanning salons, gym memberships, and fancy haircuts are not cheap, after all. (Or at least that's what I'm told— I don't consume any of these things and I sometimes even cut what little of my own hair I still have.)

The evidence is pretty strong against these ideas in the lawyer study and other studies of beauty's effect on wages, however. In the lawyer study, the pictures were taken when the subjects entered law school; so, if income causes beauty, the students would've had to be wealthy before they went to law school. But the alumni survey asked enough questions about each person's background to rule this possibility out—people who came from more privileged backgrounds were no more likely to be attractive. The evidence for any other outside factor that could cause people to be both attractive and well paid is equally lacking—there is no relationship between being attractive and being successful in ways other than income (such as, in the case of lawyers, making law review, obtaining a high class rank, or getting a judicial clerkship). All the evidence suggests that being born attractive leads to higher pay.

It looks like unattractive people get paid less, on average, for reasons completely outside their control. One could argue that this is a form of discrimination. A *Daily Show* segment on Hamermesh and his beauty research (some of the funniest and most entertaining coverage of an economist that has ever been televised) jokingly proposed that "Uglo Americans" should be a protected class of workers. But the evidence suggests that more attractive people get paid more because they are worth more, not because less attractive people are discriminated against.

It Also Pays to Be Smart and Go to School

Another attribute that people bring to both the dating and labor markets is their smarts—intelligence and knowledge. While much of what makes a person smart, interesting, and valuable (as a date or as an employee) is innate, much of it is also learned in school. As a result, education is probably the personal attribute that has been studied more widely and carefully than any other. As noted earlier, education does not appear to be directly valuable in the dating market. That is, holding other factors constant, people with more education are not more likely (or at least not much more likely) to be contacted by potential dates. Education is associated with other things, however, that make people more attractive on dating sites. Income is the most obvious of these, and the one that we will focus on. But it's worth noting that education also has other positive effects that may help a person be more attractive, such as better health.

Just as people who make more money are more sought after on dating sites, people with more education are more sought after in the labor market. The financial "returns to education" have been studied ad nauseam throughout the world, and the message is extremely consistent—more education means better jobs that pay more money.

Before we get to money, let's focus on the value of education for avoiding unemployment. In many countries, *unemployment* is defined as the fraction of all the people who want to have a job but do not have one. *Underemployment* is a looser term but a very important concept—it refers to the fraction of people who want jobs but are either not working, not working as many hours as they would like, or not able to find a job that fully utilizes their skills. No matter when or where you look, you always (and I really mean always) find that people with more education have substantially lower rates of unemployment and underemployment. For example, in the United

States in 2009 (i.e., at the height of the recession), the unemployment rate for adult men with high school degrees who did not go to college was 11 percent while the unemployment rate for adult male college graduates was 4.7 percent. But these figures understate the importance of a degree, because the underemployment rate gap was even greater.

The value of education for avoiding unemployment is not limited to recessions or the United States. In the United States, during the robust job market of 2005, only 4.7 percent of high school graduate adult males were unemployed—but college graduates were unemployed at half that rate. In Japan in 2009, the unemployment rate was 6.4 percent for men with a high school-equivalent education and only 3.1 percent for those with college-equivalent education. I have focused on men, but this same difference in unemployment (and in underemployment) is true for people of all genders, races, and ages within their own groups. More education and lower unemployment always go together.

Education's second big effect is on pay rates for those who do have jobs. Again, it does not matter where you look, when you look, or whom you look at. People with more education make more money. The exact amount extra that a person earns by staying in school varies over time and place, of course. But a good rule of thumb is that an extra year of education, other things being equal, increases pay by 8 to 10 percent. That's a lot. Going to community college, rather than stopping school after high school, leads to about 20 percent higher pay for the rest of your life. Finishing college, rather than going straight to work after high school, increases your pay by around 50 percent. Forever! And getting an MBA or a law degree is worth a substantial amount even above and beyond a college degree. Sadly, the one exception to the rule is that getting a PhD does not increase people's income relative to stopping at a master's degree.[2]

For the sake of geographic diversity, let's explore this idea by looking at some data from Australia. A recent study found that, in the early 2000s, each additional year of high school an Australian completed led to a 10 percent increase in his or her hourly wage; the final year of high school was worth a whopping 23 percent. This boost is what's known as a *sheepskin effect*—a sudden jump in income associated with completion of a degree. But the total income effects of education were even higher because more-educated Australians worked longer hours. The study also found that college graduates earned 40 percent more than high school graduates, and that those with graduate degrees earned another 15 percent more than college graduates. Others have found very similar results in, for example, Colombia and Argentina. In these countries, the fraction of the population with even a high school education is much lower, but the economic value to those who do get an education is similar to the value in Australia and other developed countries.

Sheepskin effects are very important in that they show the economic value of finishing school. So while the rule of thumb that an extra year of education increases pay by 10 percent or so is generally accurate, the increase is smaller for people who fall just short of finishing a degree. For example,

---

2. This does not mean academic economists made a bad economic decision when getting a PhD—we just have to get our utility in other ways.

someone who has completed all twelve years of secondary education will earn 16 percent more on average than someone who quits high school after junior year. But a thirteenth year of education (that is, one year of college or community college) is worth only an additional 2 percent. Similarly, finishing your junior year of college and then dropping out will not increase your pay at all relative to dropping out after sophomore year, but finishing college increases your pay by over 30 percent compared with dropping out after junior year. People have not, to my knowledge, done similar analyses of the dating market. But I suspect that, if education matters at all, its impact is due to sheepskin effects—on dating sites, people list their education by categories such as "Some College," "College Graduate," or "Graduate Degree" rather than by the number of years of school.

Does More Education Really Cause More Pay?

While you're probably convinced that people with more education make more money, you may again be thinking about causality. You may ask (in a belated attempt to impress your high school AP statistics teacher), "Does more education actually *cause* you to make more money?" It could be, for example, that smart, talented people find college and graduate school easier (making them more likely to attend) and that these same people are more productive (making them get paid more).[3] Economists have done a lot of work trying to distinguish correlation from causation in the income-education

---

3. You get bonus reader points if this made you think back to chapter 4, on signaling.

relationship. In fact, I would say that we labor economists collectively have spent about as much time on this issue as medical researchers have spent looking for a cure for cancer.[4]

The ideal way to determine whether education causes a person to make more money is to have a person stop going to school after she graduates high school, watch her career unfold for a while, then roll back the clock. Now have that same person go to college, and then see if she makes more money the second time around. Of course, while I enjoyed *Back to the Future* as much as the next guy, placing your faith in time-travel research has not proven to be successful (yet). So economists have to come up with clever ways of mimicking the time-travel method.

Researchers have separated cause and effect in education by examining the effect on income of such variables as amount of education in identical twins, age in years and months at which a child enters kindergarten, and proximity of a person's childhood home to a college campus. A critic can quibble with any one of these studies (and believe me, many a tree has given its life for papers full of such quibbling), but the body of evidence as a whole leads to a very strong conclusion—education has a large *causal* effect on income. At least for the typical person, the best way to make more money over the course of one's life is to get a good education. And for males, at least, the added income derived from increased education will help on dating sites, as well.

---

4. The good news is that we have been more successful than they have. The bad news is that we have been more successful than they have.

Tastes Change, and So Does Attractiveness

While good looks and education pay off in the dating and labor markets, demand for these attributes changes over time in both markets. What would have been considered beautiful on dating sites in the 1920s, had they existed, would be very different from what gets people noticed today. In my own case, I've been told on numerous occasions that I look like Sting. I suppose that resemblance could be attractive to some women and thus helpful in the dating market, but as Sting (and I) age that benefit will wear off. (As a side note, I was once told I look like Sting and then shortly after told that I look like David Card, a rock star among labor economists, whose research on returns to education is behind much of the discussion in this chapter. When these two resemblances were pointed out, a colleague of mine was quick to rain on the parade by noting that I sing like David Card and do economics research like Sting.)

Just as daters' tastes have changed in the last half-century, employers' taste for education has increased in recent decades. For example, from 1979 to 1987, the premium paid to college graduates relative to high school graduates increased by 30 percent. That figure has continued to grow since.

It's difficult to completely explain why the labor market rewards skills differently over time. One idea often used to explain the growing value of education is *skill-biased technical change*. That's a pretty imposing name, but the idea is simple. Over time, productivity has become affected more by ability to use technology than by mechanical and rote skills. Computers are, of course, a primary driver of this shift, but other technical change has been important as well; for example, today's car or sofa requires many fewer man-hours of construction labor than it did a few decades ago.

Globalization has contributed to and exacerbated this trend. When I worked for a high-tech company in Silicon Valley in the early 1990s, computers and computer components were produced right near the cubicle where I toiled at my marketing job. Nobody makes that type of computer equipment in the United States anymore, which has put pressure on the wages of the less-educated workers who used to build those products here.

While skill-biased technical change surely plays a part in making education more valuable, it is likely not the only factor. One piece of evidence supporting that idea is that the periods when technical change was the fastest (such as the late 1990s, when the internet blossomed) happened to coincide with periods where the value of education was *not* growing. So, like changes in fashion and trends in what works in the dating market, we can't explain everything in the labor market either.

Superstars (of Dating and Otherwise)

While the increased value of education has affected almost everyone in the labor market, there has been another change affecting only the upper extreme. Recall the dating superstar effect—the hottest 5 percent of all men get twice as many messages as the next 5 percent and several times as many messages as all other men. You may not be surprised to find out that the labor market has superstars, too. One important feature applies to both kinds of superstars—they have become more common and better compensated over time.

The rise of the superstar is another effect of technical change. In the 1950s, there were literally thousands of fairly successful stand-up comedians. A hundred years ago, there were lots of moderately successful opera singers and shoemakers. But that's not the case anymore. There are still plenty of successful comedians, but there are fewer who are moderately successful and a handful who are successful beyond the wildest dreams of the comedians of a half century ago. A great comedian of the 1950s might be successful in vaudeville or in the Catskills and travel the country playing reasonable-sized crowds. But thanks to television and the internet, Louis C.K., Jeff Foxworthy, and Chris Rock are far richer men than any of the 1950s success stories. Though many people like to go to comedy clubs, we now have the option of watching the stand-up superstars on HBO specials or Netflix. As a result, even though the superstars are only marginally more talented than the next best group of comedians out there, there is no barrier to huge audiences enjoying them simultaneously at the expense of their less-successful competitors. We can all watch the same comedians easily, and the best become superstars.

The same phenomenon applies to opera singers. In the 1800s, there were lots of opera singers playing to local audiences all around the world. But the advent of the record player, radio, and then TV turned first Maria Callas, then Joan Sutherland, and most recently the Three Tenors into unprecedentedly wealthy household names. Similarly, radio, TV, and increasing live audience capacities made the Beatles, U2, and a few others fabulously wealthy, though there were literally thousands of other rock bands active at the same time that were almost as good.

Superstars of dating can use dating sites to take advantage of the same phenomenon. If you are an extremely attractive person, you can show yourself off to many more people using Match.com and OkCupid than you could in the old days when you had to troll singles bars and meet people one at a time. I'm afraid my looks do not make me a Match.com superstar, so I have to keep working on my piano playing and my comedy act. But for my luckier peers, online dating has been a particularly fruitful development.

Uncle Sam Wants You, but Do Companies?

Men in the military get more attention on dating sites than civilian men. But do they get more attention in the labor market? After all, people learn a lot of useful skills in the military, including how to work together, stay in top physical condition, and perform some technical skills. So we might expect veterans' service to be rewarded in the labor market.

It's impossible to say whether military service is valuable in countries where it is required, such as Israel, South Korea, and Turkey, because we cannot compare people who go into the military to those who don't. But volunteer armies are problematic, too. As with education, we have to be very thoughtful about causality. In the United States, the armed forces are currently a "volunteer" group. But economist Josh Angrist recognized that the Vietnam era provided an interesting experiment. The fact that the draft lottery randomly threw some men into the military while exempting others allowed him to plausibly compare men with military service to men of similar backgrounds and abilities who were not in the military. Angrist found that, at least for white men born in the early 1950s, military service *decreased* their income by about 15 percent for at least ten years after discharge. There were no negative effects evident for minority men, however.

It's hard to say whether such a result is consistent throughout history. The Vietnam War was very unpopular in the United States, and that may have unduly hampered its veterans. Thailand currently uses a military draft lottery, so perhaps some economist will use that to study the value of military service when the current soldiers have had some experience in the labor market. As it is, economists have not yet been able to make a general statement about how military service affects people's careers.

In the End, It's Who You Know

I want to discuss one final trait that has huge economic value and pays off handsomely in the dating market, the labor market, and the business world more generally—social skills. You are nothing without the network you develop. There is an interesting difference between the way the internet has changed the value of social skills in the dating market and elsewhere, however. The internet can substitute for social skills for daters, but it enhances the value of social skills in the labor market and the business world.

I hated traditional dating. For one thing, I didn't like being set up by friends, only to have to disappoint them if the date did not go well. Like most people, I preferred to avoid work romances, but work was my primary opportunity for meeting people. Internet dating gave me a chance to meet new women and then, if it didn't work out, easily return to not knowing them. I no longer had to rely on my friends, family, and social network to find dates.

In the labor market, who you know has always mattered a great deal. Economists have only recently come to study the importance of networks in the job market and the business world, but our friends in sociology have been examining that relationship for decades. A pioneering study by Mark Granovetter in the 1970s showed something that won't shock anyone—who you know matters. Many people—in some fields, most people—get their jobs through people they know. They work for a family member, get referred by a friend, or follow a lead someone gives them at church or a club.

Internet job sites are similar to internet dating sites in their ability to bring together people and companies that would not otherwise meet. But the internet has other sites that enhance the value of the people you know and make who you know more important than it ever has been. LinkedIn's business model is built on this idea. People use LinkedIn to build and exploit their network (adding letters of reference, making connections to associates' associates, etc.) in a way that only the most organized person could have done with a Rolodex and a phone twenty years ago. Who you know has always mattered, but LinkedIn has made it possible to both know more people and better leverage those connections.

———————

Though there are many important lessons from this chapter, we are not all lucky enough to be able to take advantage of all of them. For one thing, it's really helpful to be attractive. It will get you dates and it will make you money. But if you aren't attractive, don't despair. Stay in school! Doing so will also make you more money, and in turn make you more attractive. If you are unattractive and you are really bad at school, then build your network! Get to know people, because who you know will help you get a better job. Sadly, if you are unattractive, antisocial, and don't like school, then things don't look so good right now. But *still*, don't despair—remember that tastes in the dating and labor market change over time. Perhaps we are about to start a period of "antisocial, unattractive biased technical change."

Some Things to Take Away from Chapter 9

A Key Insight from Economics: People who have a skill or attribute that is valuable to others will be compensated for it.

A Valuable or Important Empirical Finding by Economists Who Study Returns to Skill: Each extra year of education that a person completes leads to an average increase in income of about 8 to 10 percent for the rest of the person's life. — *More returns for a completed degree*

When It Comes to Returns to Skill, Dating Is a Lot Like: Getting paid for your job, going to college, trying to become the next opera superstar.

Dating Advice: Women—make yourself beautiful; men—get a raise.

10

THE FAMILY

Negotiating at Home

Though online dating is an end in itself for a few people, most of us are on dating sites to look for a long-term partner. But even when a couple settles into marriage or some other long-term relationship, economics is still very much in play. The fun is just beginning.

To see why, let's think about life on the TV show *Leave It to Beaver*, which ran in the United States during the late 1950s and early 1960s. Older readers and those who watch a lot of TV Land will remember the show's central family, the Cleavers. The Cleavers were typical of the era's television families and, to some extent, its real families. They lived in a comfortable home in the suburbs. The "man of the house," Ward Cleaver, commuted to an office where he performed some unspecified white-collar job. His wife, June, was a homemaker whose primary responsibilities were doing the family's housework and supervising the vast majority of care for the two children in the house—Wally, the older son, and his younger brother Theodore, better known as "the Beaver." The children went to school, and it was presumed that the boys would eventually pursue careers similar to their father's and suburban lives similar to their parents'.

There are still some families that resemble the Cleavers in terms of their stability and the division of labor within the household. But they are rare. If the Cleavers were a modern family, there is a good chance Ward would not live with the rest of the family, June would hold a paying job, and that either or both parents might work at home or work odd hours.

What Changed Since the Days of the Cleavers?

It might actually be simpler to ask what hasn't changed. In the United States and in other developed countries, the definition of the traditional family has rapidly evolved in response to a myriad of changes to the supply and demand of goods, services, and labor markets. At the same time, social norms have changed, at least partially as a result of economic developments, further affecting family structure. Let's start by thinking about some major economic changes that have had important effects on families.

First, the technology of home production has changed substantially in the last half-century. Put simply, it is a lot easier to keep a house in order than it used to be. Refrigeration ensures that foods can be kept longer, decreasing the amount of time that has to be spent shopping. Advances in appliances have made it less time-consuming to clean a house, cook (personally, I find it hard to believe people once got by without microwave ovens), and do laundry. Food companies developed reasonably priced and high-quality prepared foods. As a result of these changes, the time that people (OK, yes, women) used to spend housekeeping could be transferred to earning money and leisure.

At the same time, the labor market has changed. Ward Cleaver's white-collar job put him ahead of the curve. The last several decades have seen physical strength become less and less important in the labor market, a trend begun centuries ago. Human history has cast people as hunter/gatherers, then as farmers, and, by the peak of the Industrial Revolution, manufacturing workers. In each of these roles, the stronger person was also the more productive one. There are plenty of strong women out there, but, on average, men had an advantage in the workplace. Therefore, if one partner was going to stay home and the other was going out to earn a living, it usually made sense for the man to get a job outside the home.

Another important economic change (and maybe you have to be an economist to describe it that way) was the increased availability of safe birth control and abortion. Sorry to be graphic for a minute, but couples like Ward and June had sex (despite sleeping in separate beds), and before the Pill, June was likely to get pregnant pretty quickly unless Ward took actions to avoid it (which he generally wouldn't). But the advent of the birth control pill (and, to a lesser extent, abortion) allowed every woman in the same position as June Cleaver to control her own fertility. As a result, these women were more available to work outside the home if they so desired.

The final important economic change was the rise of the welfare state. In most developed countries, the state will provide some basic subsistence living (and in some countries, even more) to people with children. The benefits of such programs are often more generous for single parents, making a traditional marriage less economically valuable.

As these economic changes took place, important and related social changes did as well—possibly in response to the changing economic landscape. First, the stigma associated with being a single mother shrank substantially. Again, using the hard data of television sitcoms to prove my point, none of Beaver's friends on *Leave It to Beaver* had single mothers; if they had, they would have been treated with sympathy for the unfortunate circumstances in which they found themselves. On the other hand, modern television shows—such as *Murphy Brown*, *Friends*, and *Parenthood*—have treated children born out of wedlock as natural and relatively unremarkable plot developments.

The second social change is the increased divorce rate and decreased stigma surrounding divorce. The television show *Mad Men* depicts a suburban 1950s community similar, in many ways, to the world of *Leave It to Beaver*. But in *Mad Men* there's an explicit intolerance for deviation from the nuclear family within the community; the divorced mother in the neighborhood is ostracized and gossiped about widely. More modern communities are certainly not free from ostracism and gossip, but divorce no longer is guaranteed to be accompanied by these unpleasant side effects.

These changes have led to at least three major demographic trends—women are much more likely to hold jobs, have fewer children (or be childless altogether), and be single mothers. Consider these figures from the past half-century in the U.S. (the trends are similar in other developed countries): between 1975 and 1995, the fraction of all married women holding a job rose by more than a third (to 60 percent) and nearly doubled for those with children under three years old. The average household size dropped from 3.4 people in 1960 to 2.6 in 1995. For every 1,000 women between the ages of fifteen and forty-four, there were 118 births in 1960 against just 68 in 1980 (the rate has remained at about that level since). Nine percent of children lived with just one parent in 1960, but by 2005 that figure was 28 percent. Thirty-seven percent of the new babies in 2005 were born to unmarried women, compared with 6 percent in 1963.

Children Don't Create as Much Utility as They Used To

Now let's step back and think about how economic principles can explain how the decline in fertility and increase in women's employment is related to societal changes. Families, and especially women, have made important changes in the way they maximize their utility, spurred by the changes in the supply and/or prices of contraceptives, abortions, appliances, prepared foods, and government services.

Several of the forces mentioned have combined to increase the fraction of women who work. Essentially, the cost of working decreased and the benefits increased. First, even if June Cleaver had wanted to delay having children and instead work for a while, Ward probably would have managed to get her pregnant. Now a woman can take the Pill and be more in control of her career. Second, June's housework is—while still stressful—far easier with the advent of dishwashers, laundry machines, and prepared foods. What took June Cleaver several hours per day can now be done in much less time (hopefully, with a little contribution from Ward and maybe with a cleaning service thrown in). And while June would have had limited opportunities to work outside the home in the late 1950s, an increase in white-collar jobs has made it far easier for a comparable woman to do so today. So overall, the cost of working outside the home dropped as housework became easier, the benefits of working outside the home grew as the available jobs became more oriented toward tasks women can do well, and the Pill further reduced the cost of working outside the home by delaying child-bearing and leading to fewer children.

In economic terms, women have fewer children than they used to because the "price" of children has increased. The effect of the Pill may be best thought of the other way around—the price of avoiding children has decreased. Men's utility from sex has not changed over time, but couples can now get all the benefits associated with sex without having children. The increased relative wages of women directly increased the price of children because a woman who takes time off to tend to her children gives up more wages today than she would have in June Cleaver's time. Kids have always been costly on many levels, but their cost in terms of forgone pay has grown significantly.

OK, you say, maybe economics drives women to work more and have fewer kids, but is it really economics (rather than social changes) that has produced so many children out of wedlock? Of course! Think about an unattached woman who would like to have children. Everything else being equal, she would prefer to fall in love and share her child with a life partner. But her demand for a life partner is not as great as it would have been a few decades ago, and as a result, she is much more willing to consider raising a child by herself. Let's think about this situation separately for relatively well-off women and then for those who are less fortunate.

Professional women make more money than they did in the old days. That increase has the direct effect of making it more feasible for them to support children on their own salaries. But there's also a second, more subtle, effect of women getting richer. One good reason to have a family is that families generate economies of scale. A married couple can live together at the same level of physical comfort and at a lower cost than if the same two people lived apart. Cohabitation leads to efficiencies (you don't need twice as much space, you can share a refrigerator and a piano, and so on). But as upper-middle-class and wealthier people have gotten richer and richer in recent decades, these efficiencies have become much less important, because a given person can afford a refrigerator or a piano all by him- or herself.

But what about the less-fortunate women? Why have they become so much more likely to have children out of wedlock? Again, their fortunes in the labor market have improved. But, at least for heterosexual women, their potential partners have not been as lucky. Men with below-average skills and wages have not seen the same increases in earning power as women. In fact, at least in the United States, they actually make less money than they used to. So the benefits of having a husband have gone down (though not the benefits of having a lesbian partner).

Furthermore, if a woman from June Cleaver's era had a child out of wedlock, she would have had to fend for herself. She would have had to raise the baby using only the money that she could earn and that her family provided. Today, a single mother certainly cannot live the high life at government expense, but Aid to Families with Dependent Children, the Earned Income Tax Credit, and other welfare programs make it easier to put together at least a decent existence. Poverty of single mothers is still high, but it's much lower than it used to be. Basically, whether you are a rich or poor woman, your demand for a husband is lower than it was for the women of previous generations.

How Do Families Maximize Utility?

Now we turn from the way economics has changed the structure of families to the way it shapes the internal workings of a family. We have seen a lot of examples of how individuals make choices to try to increase their own utility. But families involve people who care about each other, so we need to now think about how decisions get made by a family member looking out for the family as a whole. A naive analysis of *Leave It to Beaver* provides a simple (but flawed) framework from which to start. Imagine a family such as the Cleavers with a husband who, in addition to earning the money, makes decisions on behalf of the household. He delegates some decisions to his wife (what to cook, for example), but he ultimately decides where the family will live, what major purchases they will make, and other important matters. He is, to be fair, a benevolent dictator, in that he makes decisions that maximize the overall household utility. In other words, he divides goods and assets among family members in such a way that, as a group, they are as happy as they could be. He's almost like a CEO who allocates resources among divisions of his company in a way that, ideally, maximizes the value of the company.

As women have gained more power in the world, that traditional model of the household has shifted. Still, it could remain the case that a head of the household or an "executive committee" makes decisions, taking the household's overall happiness into account. If this were the case, the *outcomes* of decisions made by modern couples would be the same as those made by their predecessors, except that women would be more involved in the *process*. Economists who study families describe this benevolent dictator view of families as a *common preference* model. The family is all in it together, and decisions get made the same way, no matter who makes them.

A very simple look at how partners divide housework would suggest that they do a reasonable job of maximizing overall household utility—that is, maybe this common-preference view is appropriate. For example, a utility-maximizing couple will hire a cleaning service when their own time is too valuable to spend cleaning. This could either be because they can use the time to earn more money than the cost of the cleaner, or because they have enough money to spend it on a cleaning service, effectively "buying" leisure time. But if a couple decides not to hire a cleaning service, to do their own yard work, and the like, who should do the work? The utility-maximizing couple will base the decision on two factors—who can earn more with the time that would need to be spent on the house, and who dislikes housework more. Indeed, a recent study of British couples by Leslie S. Stratton shows that couples divide up the cleaning and ironing according to who dislikes these tasks more. Men who report disliking housework less than other men do more housework. But when each gender is asked how much they like housework, men articulate a much stronger distaste, signifying that the household as a whole is happier when the woman does more of the housework.[1] Stratton concludes, "utility maximizing behavior is observed even for such mundane tasks as cleaning and laundry."

Every Spouse for Herself or Himself

Though some basic evidence suggests that households divide up the work in a way that is best for the group as a whole, the benevolent executive committee running the house efficiently turns out to be an overly altruistic view of the world that does not hold up to further scrutiny. The empirical evidence strongly rejects the benevolent dictator model. Members of a family constantly struggle and negotiate for resources. Essentially, economists have come to view families as one constant bargaining session, almost like a union sitting across the table from management. You certainly understand this idea

1. Don't blame me. The study was done by a woman.

already if you have children, since they generally are asking for more of a lot of things. (They will hopefully thank us later for not giving in to their every whim when they are young.)

But the negotiation for resources within households goes beyond kids versus parents. For example, it is well established that when one partner in a household produces new income or resources, that partner is able to garner more than his or her fair share of the new goods. The common-preference view of the world would predict that, if June Cleaver were to start working outside the home, the Cleavers would spend that money the same way they would if Ward got a raise. But that's not the way things work.

Research shows that when a woman's income increases relative to her husband's, the household spends more on restaurant meals and women's clothes and less on alcohol and tobacco. The increase in meals and clothes could simply occur because the woman now needs nicer clothes for work and has less time to cook meals at home. But the drop in alcohol and tobacco use seems to indicate that a woman who brings in more money is more empowered to tell her husband to stop wasting it.

Who *Really* Loves the Kids?

The United Kingdom created a nice opportunity to see how the distribution of income within a house affects how that money is spent. In the late 1970s, the British government changed the way it administered a child welfare subsidy. Prior to the change, the government gave a tax break to families with children that resulted in less tax being withheld from paychecks (which, at the time, primarily affected men). The tax break was replaced by a direct subsidy to the mothers of these children. One member of Parliament described this policy as a way to "take money out of the husband's pocket on Friday and put it into the wife's purse on the following Tuesday" (and he was making an argument *against* the change). The tax was a relatively clean test of how control of money affects the way it is spent, because there was no change in the actual earning of the money.

Not surprisingly, women spent some of the money on themselves. As with the studies mentioned earlier, spending on women's clothes increased. This time, however, it was clearly driven by the women's control of the money, because there was no change in how much the women worked. So when some money that used to come into a household through the man now came in through the woman, the woman spent more on clothes. That is, her bargaining power over the resources went up, and she used that shift to increase her own utility.

Now, this is not to say that partners think only of themselves. Even economists know that partners care about one another in the sense that a person's utility is higher when his or her partner is happier. However, studies such as the one on British women show that we care about our partners but we consider their happiness at least a bit less important than we consider our own.

The same statement may not apply to children, however. Most of us like to think that, as parents, we really do care as much about our children as we care about ourselves; that is, truly altruistic parents will value their child's utility just as much as they value their own. That may or may not be true, but the British study, along with many others, showed that mothers care more about their children than fathers do. When the money was given to the mother instead of to the father in Britain, she spent more on her own clothes but also more on the kids' clothes.

This finding was not just true in Britain in the late 1970s, and it also wasn't limited to children's clothes. Increases in mothers' control over family income have also been shown to increase children's health, nutrition, and even survival probabilities in developing countries. That is, children's health and happiness is a more important component of their mother's utility than it is of their father's. This discovery should not be very surprising to those of us well-versed in the theory of evolution, of course, but it is nonetheless a little emotionally jarring. Kids can—typically, at least—survive just fine if their fathers don't care about them.

Divorce Matters, Even If It Never Happens

Now that we have seen that control over resources within the family matters in determining how those resources are allocated, let's think about what other factors affect how families spend their money. You can probably think of several personality-related variables that affect who "wears the pants" in the family just based on your own experiences. But to an economist, there is one other big factor—the threat of ending the marriage. Economic models of bargaining typically find that the "outside option" is very important. That is, in business, in politics, and even in the family, a person's next-best option matters. If a woman can credibly say to her husband that he'd better shape up or she'll divorce him—and he either really loves his wife or otherwise has a lot to gain from staying married—then he's going to shape up.

Divorce is never easy or enjoyable, but the formal process has become less difficult over time. Through the 1960s, a divorce could be obtained in the United States only if one spouse did something that gave the other spouse cause to demand the end of the marriage. So unless a husband or wife could be proven to have been unfaithful or violent, or to have committed some other major transgression, a marriage could not be ended. Both spouses could agree to claim some transgression if they mutually agreed to a divorce, but this arrangement came at the cost of tarnishing one spouse's reputation and wasn't an option at all if either spouse wanted to continue the marriage.

All that changed around 1970. California led the movement to make divorce easier with the introduction of no-fault divorce, which allowed either spouse to ask for the end of the marriage for any reason. Similar rules were adopted by most other states and several other countries, including Canada and Australia.

The effects of this easing are not limited to the process itself. Think about a traditional marriage of the 1960s that is not going so well. Suppose Ward Cleaver is a lout. He goes out drinking and carousing with his friends regularly, never spends any time with Wally and the Beaver, and behaves in a way that makes June suspicious that he has a mistress. But let's suppose Ward is nevertheless happy with his marriage to June because he knows that she will keep the house clean, take care of chores, and generally make sure the kids are OK. Back in the early 1960s, there wasn't much that June could do about this situation. Not only was divorce potentially stigmatizing, threatening to leave her ostracized like the woman on *Mad Men*, but it was not even an option because this evil, alternate Ward had not committed any *proven* transgression that was grounds for divorce.

But if June Cleaver had been in the same situation in California in the 1970s, she could have gone to Ward and said, "Shape up or I'm out of here." Maybe her threat would have had no effect, and she would have had to carry through with a divorce. But if Ward valued having someone to take care of him and his children or being able to appear to be a proper family man, the advent of no-fault divorce would change the balance of power in the household even when there never ended up being a divorce. So, while no-fault divorce made divorce easier and more common, it also changed the dynamics within ongoing marriages.

Betsey Stevenson and Justin Wolfers, economists and unmarried long-term partners with children (they take their research personally), looked at how the introduction of no-fault divorce affected married couples in the United States. They compared within states before and after the introduction of no-fault divorce, while also comparing across states with and without no-fault laws at a given point in time. Rather than looking at what the couples spent money on, however, they looked at more serious outcomes—domestic violence and suicide. The results are a strong advertisement on behalf of giving women the right to divorce. Allowing a partner to exit a marriage unilaterally lowered the rates of domestic violence, murder within a marriage, and female suicide. Sadly, it appears that before no-fault divorce, some women felt that the next-best option to continuing marriage was death.

Making divorce easy does have its downsides, however, as Stevenson showed in related research. When no-fault divorce becomes the rule, a partner has less to gain by investing in the marriage. That is, if people think their spouses may leave them some day, then they have less incentive to invest in the joint benefits of marriage. Trapping partners in a marriage is a bad idea in many ways, but it does give them a reason to, for example, help each other get through college—Stevenson finds that the introduction of no-fault divorce affects couples in this manner right from the start of marriage. Couples are noticeably less likely to support each other's education when no-fault divorce is an option.

The Economics of Same-Sex Couples

Though this situation will likely change in the not-too-distant future, same-sex couples cannot legally marry in the vast majority of the world. That obstacle leads to an intra-couple negotiation dynamic that is different from the one between a married opposite-sex couple. Same-sex couples can relatively easily disband their relationship (as can cohabitating, but not married, opposite-sex couples), which makes it more risky for one member of the couple to support the other or take time off from his or her career to care for the couple's children. If a person makes sacrifices with the expectation that the other partner will repay the favor, there is always a risk of reneging that no divorce lawyer will be able to mitigate.

The economics of same-sex and opposite-sex couples are even more different when it comes to children. With very few exceptions (infertile opposite-sex couples and the rare case of lesbian couples where one partner arranges to get pregnant with a man), the cost of having children is higher for same-sex couples. Adoption, in vitro fertilization, and surrogate pregnancies are extremely expensive in terms of dollars, time, and emotional stress. In less-accepting places, the emotional costs of raising a child are also higher for same-sex couples because the parents and children can be ostracized. The extra price same-sex couples pay is surely an important factor in explaining why 60 percent of heterosexual American households have children, compared with 20 percent of lesbian and 10 percent of gay male households.

Why Do Parents Hover So Much These Days?

Even if you don't like thinking of it this way, I hope I've convinced you that the "price" of children affects how many of them we have. But you don't just have or not have children. You also have to raise them. After all (and I am not making this up), some economic papers refer to children as "consumer durable goods." Children can indeed be seen as long-term streams of costs and benefits. Think about deciding whether or not to go to your kid's Little League game (these days it's much more likely to be a soccer game, but I prefer baseball). On the one hand, you enjoy going to the game. You get positive utility from watching little Addison

(I know all of your children are Addisons), from talking to the other kids' parents, and (go ahead, you can admit it) from watching the hypercompetitive parents get into a fight. But you also pay a cost, because you could be using the time you spend at Addison's game to put in a little more work at the office, which will help you get that promotion you've been after. Or you might use the time to work out or just read a book. So how do you decide?

My parents almost never watched my Little League games. They weren't bad parents—hardly anyone's parents showed up at those games other than the coach. But I went to the vast majority of my kids' Little League games (and other sporting events) when they were in grade school. My story is no aberration. Between 1965 and 2005, the average time per week a college-educated father spent taking care of his kids went up by about five hours per week. For a college-educated mother, the increase was even greater—she spent nine more hours per week with her kids than June Cleaver did. Over-involved parents are so ubiquitous that the terms *helicopter parent* (who hovers over his children) and *tiger mom* (who incessantly drives her children to achieve) have become part of the modern middle-class suburban vocabulary.

This trend is counterintuitive, given that the "price" of time spent with kids (that is, forgone earning potential) has gone up as people have gotten wealthier. One possible reason that parents can spend more time with their kids is that, while they give up more to do so, they have a lot more money and can still buy more than the previous generation. This explanation doesn't get you very far, though, because the highest-earning college-educated parents aren't the ones who spend the most time with their kids. Another likely contributing factor is the extra time parents have as a result of technologically expedited or simply outsourced cooking, cleaning, and yard work processes. Garey Ramey and Valerey Ramey, the economists whose data on additional time spent with children appears several times above, argue that the trend is entirely due to parents trying to prepare their children to get into the most selective colleges. This explanation is not widely accepted among those who study this issue, however.

My personal best guess as to why we all spend more time watching our kids at ballet and soccer goes back to some of the game theory ideas we saw in chapter 2 and is simply a case of a *prisoner's dilemma*. If none of us take our kids' activities too seriously, we can all be seen as good parents and we can have more time available for activities that don't involve our kids. But if some parents in the area start going to the games, we worry that our kids will think we don't love them and/or will not develop properly. So there is an equilibrium where we all don't spend much time at our kids' activities, and another equilibrium where we all go to Little League games. For some reason, somewhere around 1990, the upper-middle-class suburbs of the United States shifted from the first equilibrium to the second one. Worse things can happen, though, as long as your kids aren't interested in hockey or musicals.

What Is a Modern Family?

A lot has changed in the typical family in a developed country over the last fifty years. To see those changes in action, let's end the chapter in the same scientific laboratory in which we began—American sitcoms. If *Leave It to Beaver* symbolized middle-class life in the 1960s, *Modern Family* captures the same demographic half a century later. But note the key differences. First of all, the *Modern Family* characters enjoy a much higher standard of living than the Cleavers. Educated and upper-middle-class incomes have taken off in the intervening years. Second, one household on *Modern Family* is a couple with both spouses on their second marriage, living with children from two different marriages. Another household is a gay couple with an adopted child. And finally, all the parents on the show spend what seems to be every free moment with their children. I'm not sure if they do so because they want them to get into good colleges, because of a prisoner's dilemma, or because they're able to hire cleaners and create surplus free time, but whatever drives it, there's a lot of hovering. Maybe those kids are getting a lot of benefits from all this quality time with their parents. But maybe the Beaver was better off because, thanks to June's occupation with the housekeeping, he had to learn a little independence.

Some Things to Take Away from Chapter 10

A Key Insight from Economics: The household is an economic unit like a company or a society. People bargain with each other and look out for their own interests, even at the expense of family members.

A Valuable or Important Empirical Finding by Economists Who Study the Family: If the government gives money to fathers, it's good news for breweries. If the government gives money to mothers, it's good news for makers of women's and children's clothes.

When It Comes to the Family, Dating Is a Lot Like: Dating is really just a precursor to grand bargains over who will take out the garbage.

Dating Advice: Once you've met "the one" on a dating site, don't get married until you think through what will happen if you ever break up.

EPILOGUE

Now that we have been through ten big ideas from micro-economics in some detail, it's time to step back and take stock of what we have to show for it. I'll wrap things up by summarizing how economics can help you find a partner and make online dating sites better; I'll also bring my own online dating story full circle.

Can economics really help you find a date? It may be able to help a bit, but most of what this book has discussed is *positive economics*—I've mostly just been using economics to explain the world as we observe it. For example, search theory describes how you look for mates online, but nobody can tell you when to stop looking. You have to decide when you are happy enough.

There are, though, a few useful things you can remember as you look for that special (or special enough) someone. These take us into the realm of *normative economics*—using economics to tell people how to be happier. Remember, first of all, that talk is cheap. It's easy to say that I work out every day, that I make a lot of money, and that I'm very caring (all of which are true, of course). But saying it doesn't make it so. And unfortunately, you have to remember that others know that your talk is cheap. I'm not telling you to lie or exaggerate when you describe yourself on a dating profile, but I will remind you that a lot of your competition is lying and exaggerating.

The *signaling* idea is your best alternative to the fact that talk is cheap. Make your talk expensive or, as they say, "put your money where your mouth is." Unfortunately, as we have already learned, it's hard to come up with ways to signal effectively that don't make you look weird or creepy.

I think signaling holds great potential for improving the dating market, but we're going to have to rely on the dating sites to implement opportunities for people to signal. The virtual rose experiment in Korea was an excellent start, but there are ways to take online signaling to the next level. For example, dating sites could give you the opportunity to show your interest in someone (or to show your wealth) by making a contribution to a charity on behalf of that person. Suppose you got an e-mail from your online dating service that said, "Mick349 has donated $10 to the Springfield Soup Kitchen on your behalf. Check out his profile at . . . " You would probably check the guy's profile out and give him a chance, wouldn't you? This could also be an opportunity to show you truly believe in something—imagine receiving a message reading, "Mick349 has donated $10 to the [choose one of: National Rifle Association, Planned Parenthood, the Democratic National Committee, the Tea Party] on your behalf. Check out his profile." If he picked the right place to send his money, it might be very impressive. You might take the signal seriously because it was costly—he put his money where his mouth is.

The *adverse selection* idea reinforces some dating advice that you probably already knew intuitively—if someone has not had a serious relationship or has had lots and lots of short relationships, there's probably a reason. Now, far be it from me to recommend that anyone statistically discriminate (and you women out there should definitely go easy on the separated men). But when your mother told you "Where there's smoke, there's fire," she was trying to teach you about adverse selection, and you should probably listen.

In the end, the best advice I or any economist can provide is that you have to be in the market to succeed in the market. I used multiple dating sites, I was very open-minded about the types of women I would go on first dates with (OK, maybe not *very* open-minded, but open-minded enough), and I tried to be basically honest (with the few minor caveats I confessed to in chapter 2). I looked for bigger dating sites (thicker markets) and only limited my options based on criteria that were very important to me.

And, I'm happy to report, it all paid off. After many first dates, lots of multiple-date relationships that did not go anywhere, and one six-month relationship, I e-mailed "Profunny" on JDate. JDate is a Jewish dating site. Now, you might not think this was a place I should have been looking, given that I was narrowing the market down (using a thinner market) in a way that was not important to me. I am technically and culturally Jewish. I give my children Hanukkah, rather than

Christmas, presents. But I am not religious, I am not a devout Jew (I had to look up how to spell Hanukkah when I wrote the last sentence), and I don't much care whether my partner is Jewish or not. But there are a lot of very smart, educated Jewish women in my geographic area, so JDate was a thick market for the type of woman I was hoping to meet.

It turned out that Profunny, who now allows me to call her Kathryn, works one hundred yards from my office, that her JDate name accurately describes her sense of humor, and that she was delightful when we eventually met at Cafe Borrone (my go-to first-date spot all through my online dating experiences). We got to know each other and to really like each other so that when we revealed our secrets (you know mine, which at the time included that I was writing a book about online dating; hers were highlighted by her two unimaginably ridiculous pugs), they were easy to overcome. Rational economist that I am, I'll leave it at that and spare you the details about giving flowers, going together to the Shakespeare festival, taking long walks hand-in-hand, falling in love, etc. Suffice it to say that I quickly realized that the benefits of sticking with her clearly outweighed those of trying to trade up. I know this for two reasons. First, she read chapter 1 (on search theory) and didn't immediately peg me as heartless and dump me. Second, my teenage daughter, reinforcing my ego as always, told me never to break up with Kathryn because she is "out of your league."

And so now, if you don't already have that special someone, it's your turn to hit the market. And if you already have that special someone, I hope you'll start applying the ideas in this book to see the economics in everyday life all around you all the time. Think about it as you shop, as you play sports (economics drives your decision to hit a tennis serve soft or hard, for example), when you watch pro sports (should the penalty kick go left or right?), and when you watch a movie (I recommend *Trading Places*—hard to beat the combination of entertainment and economics lessons in one two-hour package). And may all your adventures maximize your utility.

NOTES

Chapter 1

9: *Nick Paumgarten's online dating story:* "Looking for Someone," *New Yorker*, July 4, 2011.

12: *Young Chinese woman's online profile:* Quoted in Evan Osnos, "The Love Business," *New Yorker*, May 14, 2012.

14: *Lori Gottlieb quotes:* Lori Gottlieb, "Marry Him!" *The Atlantic*, March 2008 and Lori Gottlieb, *Marry Him: The Case for Settling for Mr. Good Enough* (New York: Dutton, 2010).

15: *"I tire of articles . . . ":* From "jh40" on http://www.theatlantic.com/magazine/archive/2008/03/marry-him/6651/#.

17–18: *Nobel Prize committee quote:* nobelprize.org.

19–21: *Study of New York State pharmacies:* Alan Sorensen, "Equilibrium Price Dispersion in Retail Markets for Prescription Drugs," *Journal of Political Economy* 108 (August 2000): 833–850.

22: *Study of older people's shopping habits:* Mark Aguiar and Erik Hurst, "Life-Cycle Prices and Production," *American Economic Review* 97, no. 5 (December 2007): 1533–1559.

Chapter 2

27: *Background on cooperative game theory:* See Thomas C. Schelling, *The Strategy of Conflict* (Cambridge, MA: Harvard University Press, 1981).

27: *Non-technical overview of cheap talk:* See Joseph Farrell and Matthew Rabin, "Cheap Talk," *Journal of Economics Perspectives* 10 (1996): 103–118.

28: *Studies documenting lying on dating sites:* Jeffrey T. Hancock, Catalina Toma, and Nicole Ellison, "The Truth About Lying in Online Dating Profiles," *CHI 2007 Proceedings* (2007): 449–452; and Christian Rudder, "The Big Lies People Tell in Online Dating," OKCupid blog, July 10, 2010, http://blog.okcupid.com/index.php/the-biggest-lies-in-online-dating/.

32: *Study of economists lying on their résumés:* Christopher Snyder and Owen Zidar, "Resume Padding by Economists," working paper, Dartmouth College, 2011.

37: *Study of fresh snow reports at ski areas:* Jonathan Zinman and Eric Zitzewitz, "Wintertime for Deceptive Advertising?" working paper, Dartmouth College, 2012.

38–39: *Studies of cheap talk by executives and securities analysts:* Jeremy C. Stein, "Efficient Capital Markets, Inefficient Firms: A Model of Myopic Corporate Behavior," *Quarterly Journal of Economics* 104 (1989): 655–669; Harrison Hong and Jeffrey D. Kubik, "Analyzing the Analysts: Career Concerns and Biased Earnings Forecasts," *Journal of Finance* 58 (2003): 313–351; and Hsiou-wei Lin and Maureen F. McNichols, "Underwriting Relationship, Analysts' Earnings Forecasts, and Investment Recommendations," *Journal of Accounting and Economic* 25 (February 1998): 101–127.

39–40: *Discussion of the Federal Reserve:* Based on Jeremy C. Stein, "Cheap Talk and the Fed: A Theory of Imprecise Policy Announcements," *American Economic Review* 79 (1989): 32–42.

41: *Model of cheap talk by politicians:* Joseph Harrington, "The Revelation of Information through the Electoral Process: An Exploratory Analysis," *Economics and Politics* 4 (1992): 255–276.

Chapter 3

57–58: *Details on the London congestion rules and traffic:* "Congestion Charge Cuts Jams," *BBC News*, June 6, 2003, http://news.bbc.co.uk/2/hi/uk_news/2967852.stm.

Chapter 4

64: *Original article on signaling:* Michael Spence, "Job Market Signaling," *Quarterly Journal of Economics* 87 (1973): 355–374.

64: *Analysis of the roses on the Korean site:* Soohyung Lee, Muriel Niederle, Hye-Rim Kim, and Woo-Keum Kim, "Propose with a Rose? Signaling in Internet Dating Markets," working paper, Stanford University, 2011.

66–67: *Study of signals on the economist job market:* Peter Coles, John Cawley, Philip B. Levine, Muriel Niederle, Alvin E. Roth, and John J. Siegfried, "The Job Market for New Economists: A Market Design Perspective," *Journal of Economic Perspectives* 24, no. 4 (Fall 2010): 187–206.

67–68: *David Sedaris on immigration process:* "Long Way Home," *New Yorker*, April 1, 2013.

77: *Quotes on University of Chicago's application process:* Scott Jaschik, "Chicago Students Rally to Be Uncommon," *Inside HigherEd*, December 1, 2006.

79: *Study showing the value early decision:* Christopher Avery and Jonathan Levin, "Early Admissions at Selective Colleges," *American Economic Review* 100 (December 2010): 2125–2156.

79–80: *Mildred's (the GED earner) story:* http://www.youtube.com/watch?v=l53sHBekvOY&feature=plcp&context=C4a4a708VDvjVQa1Ppc FOvBO0oB_pE5B2DTkTDZbbPJ1G8qbaWgKM%3D.

80: *Income figures for high school dropouts and graduates:* US Census Bureau, reported in *The High Cost of High School Dropouts*, (Washington, DC: Alliance for Excellent Education, 2007).

80–81: *Evidence on the cost of earning a GED:* Stephen V. Cameron and James J. Heckman, "The Nonequivalence of High School Equivalents," *Journal of Labor Economics* 11 (1993): 1–47.

81–82: *Study of the GED as a signal:* John H. Tyler, Richard J. Murnane, and John B. Willett, "Estimating the Labor Market Signaling Value of the GED," *Quarterly Journal of Economics* 115 (2000): 431–468.

83: *Strategies recommended by the Chinese adviser:* Evan Osnos, "The Love Business," *New Yorker*, May 14, 2012.

87: *Discussions about LinkedIn's IPO:* Joe Nocera, "Was LinkedIn Scammed?" *New York Times*, May 20, 2011; and Andrew Ross Sorkin, "Why LinkedIn's Price May Have Been Right," *New York Times*, May 23, 2011.

Chapter 5

100: *John Ashcroft quotes:* "Fact Sheet: Racial Profiling" (Washington, DC: US Department of Justice, June 17, 2003), available at http://www.justice.gov/opa/pr/2003/June/racial_profiling_fact_sheet.pdf.

100: *EEOC definition of discriminatory practices:* http://www.eeoc.gov/facts/qanda.html.

104–108: *The academic studies, in the order discussed, are:*

Joseph G. Altonji and Charles R. Pierret, "Employer Learning and Statistical Discrimination," *Quarterly Journal of Economics* 116 (2001): 313–350.

Ian Ayres and Peter Siegelman, "Race and Gender Discrimination in Bargaining for a New Car," *American Economic Review* 85 (1995): 304–321.

John A. List, "The Nature and Extent of Discrimination in the Marketplace: Evidence from the Field," *Quarterly Journal of Economics* 119 (2004): 49–89.

Asaf Zussman, "Ethnic Discrimination: Evidence from the Israeli Online Market for Used Cars," *Economic Journal*, forthcoming.

Jennifer L. Doleac and Luke C. D. Stein, "The Visible Hand: Race and Online Market Outcomes," working paper, Stanford University, 2010.

Chapter 6

115: *Study of job mobility and metropolitan area size:* Hoyt Bleakley and Jeffrey Lin, "Thick-Market Effects and Churning in the Labor Market: Evidence from U.S. Cities," *Journal of Urban Economics* 72 (2012): 87–103.

116–117: *Where gay people live:* Dan A. Black, Seth G. Sanders, and Lowell J. Taylor, "The Economics of Lesbian and Gay Families," *Journal of Economic Perspectives* 21 (2007): 53–70.

118: *Study on lawyer specialties and market thickness:* Luis Garicano and Thomas N. Hubbard, "Specialization, Firms, and Markets: The Division of Labor within and between Law Firms," *Journal of Law, Economics, and Organization* 25 (2009): 339–371.

118: *Study of business outsourcing and market size:* Yukako Ono, "Market Thickness and Outsourcing Services," *Regional Science and Urban Economics* 37 (2007): 220–238.

119–120: *Stores in the Lighting District:* Maya Pope-Chappell, "Lights Out on the Bowery," http://online.wsj.com/article/SB1000142405311 1903520204576481973812283848.html.

120–121: *Original Hotelling article:* Harold Hotelling, "Stability in Competition," *Economic Journal* 39 (1929): 41–57.

122: *Carbon black industry:* H. Allen Anderson, "Carbon Black Industry," *Handbook of Texas Online*, http://www.tshaonline.org/handbook/online/articles/doc01.

122–123: *Wine industry data:* US Department of the Treasury statistics, available at http://www.ttb.gov/statistics/2009_wine_calendar_year.pdf.

123–124: *Dalton, GA carpeting business:* Numerous sources, including Randall L. Patton, "A History of the U.S. Carpet Industry," EH.net encyclopedia, February 4, 2010, http://eh.net/encyclopedia/article/patton.carpet.

124: *Historical industries in Detroit:* Mike Brewster, "Billy Durant: Greasing Detroit's Wheels," *Bloomberg Businessweek*, April 26, 2004, http://www.businessweek.com/stories/2004-04-26/billy-durant-greasing-detroits-wheels; and Edward Glaeser, "Can Detroit Find the Road Forward?" *New York Times* Econimix blog, February 22, 2011, http://economix.blogs.nytimes.com/2011/02/22/can-detroit-find-the-road-forward/.

125–126: *Analysis of gastroenterologists:* Muriel Niederle and Alvin E. Roth, "Unraveling Reduces Mobility in a Labor Market: Gastroenterology with and without a Centralized Match," *Journal of Political Economy* 111 (2003): 1342–1352.

128–129: *Analysis of law clerks:* Christopher Avery, Christine Jolls, Richard A. Posner, and Alvin E. Roth, "The New Market for Federal Judicial Law Clerks," *University of Chicago Law Review* 74 (2007): 447–486.

Chapter 7

131: *Quotes on the stigma of online and computer dating:* Jennifer Egan, "Love in the Time of No Time," *New York Times*, November 23, 2003.

132–133: *Akerlof's seminal paper on adverse selection:* George A. Akerlof, "The Market for 'Lemons': Quality Uncertainty and the Market Mechanism," *Quarterly Journal of Economics* 84 (1970): 488–500.

135: *Quotes about the stigma of being unemployed while job-hunting:* Catherine Rampell, "The Help-Wanted Sign Comes with a Frustrating Asterisk," *New York Times*, July 25, 2011.

135–136: *Study on the stigma of being the victim of downsizing:* Robert Gibbons and Lawrence Katz, "Layoffs and Lemons," *Journal of Labor Economics* 9 (1991): 351–380.

139: *Quotes on AAirpass:* Ken Bensinger, "The Frequent Fliers Who Flew Too Much," *Los Angeles Times*, May 5, 2012.

139: *Additional details on the AAirpass program:* Brad Tuttle, "The $250,000 Airline Pass That Was Worth Every Penny," *Time*, May 8, 2012.

140–141: *Capital One story:* Garth Saloner and Victoria Chang, "Capital One Financial Corporation: Setting and Shaping Strategy," Stanford Graduate School of Business Case Study, (Stanford, CA: Stanford Graduate School of Business, 2004).

144: *Safelite's pay-for-performance plan:* Edward P. Lazear, "Performance Pay and Productivity," *American Economic Review* 90 (2000): 1346–1361; and Brian J. Hall, Carleen Madigan, and Edward Lazear, "Performance Pay at Safelite Auto Glass" (A) and (B), Harvard Business School Case Studies (Boston: Harvard Business Publishing, 2000).

146: *The blogger commentary on Volvo drivers:* http://mistyhorizon2003. hubpages.com/hub/Volvo-Drivers-and-Why-They-are-Dangerous.

Chapter 8

153: *Figures on college and married couples:* Christine R. Schwartz and Robert D. Mare, "Trends in Educational Assortative Marriage from 1940 to 2003," *Demography* 42 (November 2005): 621–646.

154: *Statistics on commonality of traits of married and other committed couples:* Lisa K. Jepsen and Christopher A. Jepsen, "An Empirical Analysis of the Matching Patterns of Same-Sex and Opposite-Sex Couples," *Demography* 39 (August 2002): 435–453.

155: *Positive assortative mating by parental education and its increase over time:* Elaina Rose, "Marriage and Assortative Mating: How Have the Patterns Changed?" working paper, University of Washington, 2001.

156: *Analysis of British social class migration:* Jo Blanden, Paul Gregg, and Stephen Machin, *Intergenerational Mobility in Europe and North America*, London School of Economics report to the Sutton Trust, 2005.

157: *Henry Moore findings and quotes:* Henry L. Moore, *Laws of Wages* (New York: Macmillan, 1911), as quoted by Walter Y. Oi and Todd L. Idson, "Firm Size and Wages," *Handbook of Labor Economics*, vol. 3, ed. by Orley C. Ashenfelter and David Card (Amsterdam/New York: Elsevier, 1999); *Handbook of Labor Economics* is the source of all figures in this paragraph.

159: *Analysis of productivity and firm size in France:* John M. Abowd, Francis Kramarz, and David N. Margolis, "High Wage Workers and High Wage Firms," *Econometrica* 67 (February 1999): 251–333.

159: *Similar Swiss study:* Rudolf Winter-Ebmer and Josef Zweimuller, "Firm-Size Wage Differentials in Switzerland: Evidence from Job-Changers," *American Economic Review* (AEA Papers and Proceedings) 89 (May 1999): 89–93.

162: *Garment factory analysis:* Barton H. Hamilton, Jack A. Nickerson, and Hideo Owan, "Team Incentives and Worker Heterogeneity: An Empirical Analysis of the Impact of Teams on Productivity and Participation," *Journal of Political Economy* 111, no. 3 (2003): 465–497.

162–163: *Analysis of students stuffing envelopes:* Armin Falk and Andrea Ichino, "Clean Evidence on Peer Effects," *Journal of Labor Economics* 24, no. 1 (2006): 39–57.

163–164: *Supermarket checker study:* Alexandre Mas and Enrico Moretti, "Peers at Work," *American Economic Review* 99, no. 1 (2009): 112–145.

166: *One study that finds classroom peer effects in Belgium, the United States, Canada, France, and New Zealand:* Ron W. Zimmer and Eugenia F. Toma, "Peer Effects in Private and Public Schools Across Countries," *Journal of Policy Analysis and Management* 19 (1999): 75–92. Other studies find them in other countries, as well.

166: *Studies of positive assortative mating in other animals:* Jeffrey G. Groth, "Call Matching and Positive Assortative Mating in Red Crossbills," *The Auk* 110 (1993): 398–401; Gudbjorg Olafsdottir, Michael G. Ritchie, and Sigurdur S. Snorrason, "Positive Assortative Mating Between Recently Described Sympatric Morphs of Icelandic Sticklebacks," *Biology Letters* 2 (June 2006): 250–252; and Goran Arnqvist, Locke Rowe, James J. Krupa, and Andy Sih, "Assortative Mating by Size: A Meta-Analysis of Mating Patterns in Water Striders," *Evolutionary Ecology* 10 (1996): 265–284.

Chapter 9

169–170: *Analyses of preferences on dating sites:* Gunter Hitsch, Ali Hortacsu, and Dan Ariely, "What Makes You Click? Mate Preferences in Online Dating," *Quantitative Marketing and Economics* 8, no. 4 (December 2010): 393–427; Christian Rudder, "The Mathematics of Beauty," OKCupid blog, http://blog.okcupid.com/index.php/the-mathematics-of-beauty/; and Soohyung Lee, "Marriage and Online Mate-Search Services: Evidence from South Korea," 2009, working paper, University of Maryland.

173–174: *Studies of how looks and weight are related to income:* Daniel S. Hamermesh and Jeff E. Biddle, "Beauty and the Labor Market," *American Economic Review* 84 (1994): 1174–1194; John Cawley, "The Impact of Obesity on Wages," *Journal of Human Resources* 39 (2004): 451–474; and Jeff E. Biddle and Daniel S. Hamermesh, "Beauty, Productivity, and Discrimination: Lawyers' Looks and Lucre," *Journal of Labor Economics* 16 (1998): 172–201.

177–178: *Figures on US employment:* Bureau of Labor Statistics tables, available at www.bls.gov.

178: *Figures on Japanese employment:* http://www.oecd.org/japan/48657354.pdf.

179: *Australian returns to education figures:* Andrew Leigh, "Returns to Education in Australia," *Economic Papers* 27 (September 2008): 233–249.

179: *Discussion of Colombia and Argentina:* Marco Manacorda, Carolina Sanchez-Paramo, and Norbert Schady, "Changes in Returns to Education in Latin America: The Role of Demand and Supply of Skills," *Industrial and Labor Relations Review* 68 (January 2010): 307–326.

179–180: *Discussion of sheepskin effects:* David A. Jaeger and Marianne E. Page, "Degrees Matter: New Evidence on Sheepskin Effects in the Returns to Education," *Review of Economics and Statistics* 78 (November 1996): 733–740.

182: *Discussion of how the returns to education have changed over time:* Lawrence F. Katz and Kevin M. Murphy, "Changes in Relative Wages 1963–1987: Supply and Demand Factors," *Quarterly Journal of Economics* 107 (February 1992): 35–78; and Lawrence F. Katz and David H. Autor, "Changes in the Wage Structure and Earnings Inequality," *Handbook of Labor Economics*, vol. 3, ed. by Orley C. Ashenfelter and David Card (Amsterdam/New York: Elsevier, 1999)

184: *Economic analysis of superstars:* First spelled out in Sherwin Rosen, "The Economics of Superstars," *American Economic Review* 71 (1981): 845–858.

185–186: *Study of the effects of military service on income:* Joshua D. Angrist, "Lifetime Earnings and the Vietnam Era Draft Lottery: Evidence from the Social Security Administration Records," *American Economic Review* 80 (1990): 313–336.

186: *Thai draft lottery:* Janasera Fugal, "Thai Military Draft a Lottery Many Hope to Lose," *Dawn*, April 16, 2011.

187: *Importance of contacts in finding a job:* Mark S. Granovetter, *Getting a Job: A Study of Contracts and Careers* (Cambridge, MA: Harvard University Press, 1974).

Chapter 10

192: *Statistics on women in the workforce, number of children, and single mothers:* V. Joseph Hotz, Jacob Alex Klerman, and Robert J. Willis, "The Economics of Fertility in Developed Countries," *Handbook of Population and Family Economics*, ed. Mark R. Rosenzweig and Oded Stark (Amsterdam/New York: Elsevier, 1997); and Shelly Lundberg and Robert A. Pollak, "The American Family and Family Economics," *Journal of Economic Perspectives* 21 (2007): 3–26.

198: *Study of how British couples divide housework:* Leslie S. Stratton, "The Role of Preferences and Opportunity Costs in Determining the Time Allocated to Housework," *American Economic Review* (AEA Papers and Proceedings) 102 (May 2012): 606–611.

199–200: *Study of how British couples' spending patterns changed when child benefits were shifted from the father to the mother:* Shelly J. Lundberg, Robert A. Pollak, and Terence J. Wales, "Do Husbands and Wives Pool Their Resources? Evidence from the United Kingdom Child Benefit," *Journal of Human Resources* 32 (1997): 463–480.

202–203: *Positive effect of no-fault divorce on divorce rates:* Leora Friedberg, "Did Unilateral Divorce Raise Divorce Rates? Evidence from Panel Data," *American Economic Review* 88 (1998): 608–627.

203–204: *Studies of effect of no-fault divorces on married couples:* Betsey Stevenson and Justin Wolfers, "Bargaining in the Shadow of the Law: Divorce Laws and Family Distress," *Quarterly Journal of Economics* 121 (2006): 267–288; and Betsy Stevenson, "The Impact of Divorce Laws on Marriage-Specific Human Capital," *Journal of Labor Economics* 25 (2007): 75–94.

205: *Figures on children in heterosexual and same-sex households:* Dan A. Black, Seth G. Sanders, and Lowell J. Taylor, "The Economics of Lesbian and Gay Families," *Journal of Economic Perspectives* 21 (2007): 53–70.

207: *Changes in time spent with children:* Garey Ramey and Valerie A. Ramey, "The Rug Rat Race," *Brookings Papers on Economic Activity* (Washington, DC: Brookings Institution, 2010): 129–199.

INDEX

ACKNOWLEDGMENTS

I want to start by thanking all the women I dated in 2010, 2011, and 2012. I did not generally know at the time that they were "data" for this project, but they turned out to be invaluable.

I am grateful for the encouragement I got from many people with whom I discussed this book and who read drafts of chapters along the way, including Mike Mazzeo, Enrico Moretti, Jack Repcheck, Scott Schaefer, Deborah Simon-Lurie, Lizzie Skurnick, and Alan Sorensen.

My agent, Zoe Pagnamenta, has been a wonderful teacher of how to write, how to appeal to the audience that might read this book, and how to work with the publishing industry. She was always encouraging, had some great ideas, and was very diligent. The book would not have happened without her.

My editor, Tim Sullivan, was a tremendous support when this book was just a glimmer of an idea. His encouragement kept me motivated and his input on early drafts was critical.

The biggest contributor to this book (other than me, I hope) was Sara Klein. After my first date back in the fall of 2010, I wrote her an e-mail telling her some of the stories about it, and she replied, in part, "You need to keep records of all this so you can write a book. It'll have a math-y flavor and it will be about efficiency in dating, or something like that. It has a happy ending." There's no math in this book, but I otherwise followed her suggestion pretty carefully. Sara also read the chapters as they were written. I cannot thank her enough for her input and faith in this. She made me believe people would actually want to read this.

This is going to sound silly, but I want to thank my dogs. When I started dating in 2010, my golden retriever, Opus, was my sidekick and companion. He was both my best asset and my biggest impediment on the dating market. He was also great to come home to after another lousy date, and he was happy and playful while women ignored me or rejected me. He was truly my best friend but, sadly, he passed away in the early stages of this project. His successor, Josie, has been a great source of distraction as I wrote. I had many of my best insights for this book while walking both of them. But, more importantly, Opus and Josie have to be the most optimistic and fun-loving creatures who ever lived. That blind "Wow, this seems great!" attitude is something I always try to emulate. I look forward to Josie eating a few copies of this book and wish Opus were here to join her.

As noted in the epilogue, the best thing to come out of my online dating experience was meeting my significant other, Kathryn Stoner. In addition to being really grateful that she puts up with me in general, I thank her for her encouragement, her helpful discussion of the ideas in this book, and her valuable input on draft chapters. I sure hope she continues to resist the temptation to trade up in the boyfriend market.

And finally, I want to thank my family. My children, David and Lucy, make all the effort that went into this book and everything else worthwhile. I hope that having their father dating again hasn't been too embarrassing and that they can forgive me for now telling the whole world about it. I am also grateful to David for doing an excellent job editing the final manuscript. Finally, I want to thank my parents for everything they have done for me over the years that made this book, and everything that led up to it, possible. My father's work ethic has always been an inspiration—I could not have completed a project like this without the drive he taught me. My late mother, Alice Oyer, taught me so many things related to this book, especially the most un-economic concept of all—unconditional love. I will always miss her. I dedicate this book to her, knowing that she'd be proud of me for it, even though it's a silly book about online dating.

ABOUT THE AUTHOR

Paul Oyer is the Fred H. Merrill Professor of Economics at Stanford University's Graduate School of Business. He is also a Research Associate with the National Bureau of Economic Research and the Editor-in-Chief of the *Journal of Labor Economics*. He lives in Stanford, California, with his two children and his flat-coated retriever, Josie.